DEMOCRACY'S DILEMMA

DEMOCRACY'S DILEMMA

The Challenges to State Legitimacy in

Afghanistan

DAVID SHAMS

Published by Lulu.com

ISBN: 978-1-4357-1101-3
LCCN: 2008901643

To my wife

Acknowledgements

I would like to thank my wife, who diligently read and edited this book a million times. While assisting me with research and organization, she offered great moral support and encouragement, for which I am grateful. It is also difficult to find words with which I could express gratitude to my professors for their guidance throughout the process of writing this book. Moreover, many thanks to my wonderful children for generously donating hundreds of precious "play-time" hours to this project.

Contents

Chapter		Page
One	**Introduction**	1
Two	**Statehood and Legitimacy**	4
	Standards of Statehood	5
	The Legitimate State	6
	Coercion or Persuasion?	8
	Monopoly on Violence	10
	Conclusion	11
Three	**The Struggle to Assert Legitimacy**	12
	What is Legitimacy?	14
	State Formation	16
	Conclusion	16
Four	**Joya and the Warlords: Past Crimes and Contemporary Politics**	18
	A Brief History	19
	Mujaheddin or Warlords?	19
	Testimonies and Evidence	20
	The Unforgotten Past	21
	Ittihaad	24
	Wahdat	26
	Hezb e Islami	27
	Jamiat	28
	Junbesh e Melli	28
	History of Crimes and Violence	29
	Assessing Accountability	30
	Afghans Demand Justice	32

Trust, Respect and Legitimacy   35
Conclusion   37

Five   **Reconciliation and Appeasement: Why Are the Taliban and Warlords Able to Participate in Afghanistan's Democratic Process?**   39

Who is back in power?   40
Abdul Rab Rasul Sayyaf   42
Abdul Rashid Dostam   43
Fahim Qasim   44
Hazrat Ali   46
Reconciliation or Regression to Chaos?   46
The Struggle to Survive   49
The U.S. Foreign Policy   50
Conclusion   51

Six   **Corruption and Drugs: A Deadly Combination Weakening the State**   53

Institutional Corruption   54
Lack of Accountability   55
Law Enforcement   56
Conclusion   63

Seven   **Impact of Drug Trade on State Legitimacy**   64

Disparity   66
Inequality   69
Dependency   70
Conclusion   73

Works Cited   75

CHAPTER ONE

Introduction

The idea of writing this book occurred to me after writing a paper during my graduate studies in which I questioned warlords' and the Taliban's participation in Afghanistan's democratic process. Soon after, I decided to expand on the same topic, and examine the effects of warlords' deep involvement in the makeup of the current government and on the legitimacy of the state.

I began my research by studying news articles and papers in academic journals as well as books published by prominent scholars and journalists who have extensively studied Afghan politics. Many have also traveled to Afghanistan and throughout the region, conducted research and served in governmental and nongovernmental organizations. As a result, I discovered that three main elements have hindered the process of reconstruction and reform, as well as the formation of a legitimate state in Afghanistan: human rights violations, institutional corruption, and drug cultivation and trade. All three elements have stemmed from the methods and the policies that the state has assumed in an effort to succeed in the reconciliatory process with the warring factions. The state has taken these measures to prevent the recurrence of another armed conflict between the state and the warlords, which could easily lead to chaos and political destabilization throughout the country.

Analysis and assessments by political scientists are not the only sources that point to the obscurity of issues that the Afghan state has to face in order to achieve legitimacy among the Afghans, and to protect its territorial and political sovereignty. Various media reports also draw similar conclusions about the challenges that Afghanistan has had to grapple with since the fall of the Taliban. The state has dealt with difficulties beyond the resurgence of the Taliban and regrouping of Al Qaeda. Afghan media such as Pazwok News Service and Kabul Press, as well as, the non-Afghan media such as the New York Times, Washington Post and Christian Science Monitor have emphasized the complexity of the issues in which the Afghan state continuously finds itself entangled.

In addition to these sources, I have also used the findings of studies conducted by reputable international organizations. These reports contain tremendously helpful data in assessing the gravity and comprehending the intricacy of various social, political and economic matters in Afghanistan. Among many, "Afghanistan Opium Survey 2006" published by the United Nations Office on Drugs and Crime (UNODC) serves as great example. This organization has conducted far-reaching research on the different aspects of opium economy and the various manners in which it has affected the Afghan state and society. For example, it offers statistical data in regards to the annual cultivation of poppy as well as the decrease and or increase of its yield in many parts of the country. The report presents a comparative study of the rise and fall in opium supply and prices. It also provides critical information about the socio-economic ramifications of opium production and trade. This book will present some of these findings while analyzing the relationship between drug trade and corruption.

Human Rights Watch (HRW) has also conducted extensive research about the gross human rights violations allegedly committed by warlords. The study has focused on war crimes committed during the 1992-1993 period - after the fall of the Marxist regime in Afghanistan. It is therefore accordingly titled "Blood Stained Hands: Past Atrocities in Kabul, and Afghanistan's Legacy of Impunity." Reports as such help the reader appreciate not only the gravity of the horrendous war crimes of the past, but also their significance in terms of their continuing impact on the contemporary Afghan politics. This comprehension is extraordinarily important because the participation of alleged war criminals in the current political process plays an imperative role in shaping people's perception of the state and its legitimacy.

Human Rights Watch describes itself as an independent organization free of political and economic attachments to any governmental or non-governmental organization. Through conducting research on human rights abuses and war crimes in Afghanistan, its goal is to provide a verifiable and legitimate account of the atrocities committed during these years. In the process of an intensive fact finding campaign, its researchers interviewed hundreds of Kabul's residents whom have seen the street battles in the city, and or fallen victim to atrocities of war.

"A Call for Justice" is the title of another study, which has played a key role in writing this book. The Afghan Independent Human Rights Commission (AIHRC) has prepared this report. The formation of this organization is the result of the sixth article of the Bonn agreement, which insisted on the creation of a neutral entity to draw a road map for the process of transitional justice. As a whole, this document is the result of thousands of interviews with 4151 civilians throughout the country, as well as 1300 Afghan refugees in India, and an additional 400 in Pakistan. Researchers conducted these interviews from January to August 2004. The point noteworthy about this study is that in addition to providing the reader with statistics, charts, and tables, it directly quotes the public's opinions and describes their experiences during the dark days of the civil war. This helps one better understand the human rights conditions in the context of Afghanistan's contemporary political history.

However, my efforts in finding reliable sources have not been limited to news stories published by reputable publications, nor has it been confined to the results of research conducted by highly regarded international organizations. I have also used analysis, statements, and speeches by key scholars, prominent politicians, and renowned leaders such as Hamed Karzai, Zalmai Khalilzad, Antonio Costa, and Barnet Rubin in regards to human rights, economic development, drug trade and the impact of corruption on the state building process and democratization in Afghanistan.

Furthermore, in an attempt to distinguish the definition of the *state* from that of a *legitimate* state, I have taken advantage of writings by many classical as well as modern political theorists such as Max Weber, Joel Migdal, Ashraf Ghani, John Schar, Henri Claessen, Robert Jackson and Carl Rosberg. This is important since both concepts - statehood and legitimacy constitute the central theme of this project. My objective is to assess the degree to which the current political institution can hold claim to legitimacy.

Warlords' participation in the current political process has profoundly affected the lives of Afghans in various manners. Their ability to capture and hold high-ranking positions in the government apparatus has shaped Afghanistan's newly formed political structures and nascent developing economy. This seems primarily the consequence of a political formula that directly influences the process of state formation.

Because of a yearlong research, I have discovered facts that have helped me better comprehend and analyze the relative nature of matters such as drug trade, corruption, and human rights abuses and their relation to each other. Nevertheless, considering the scope of the issue of legitimacy within the intricate political and economic realities of Afghanistan, it is much likely that I have not been able to touch upon all factors at play. In this book, I have chosen to write selectively and specifically about those facets of the current political trends that directly relate to the role of warlords in the process of state formation and legitimization in Afghanistan.

CHAPTER TWO

Statehood and Legitimacy

Through a careful review of the literature surrounding statehood and the issue of legitimacy, one easily realizes that there exists a distinction between the definition of the state and that of its legitimacy. The state is a political institution comprised of smaller sub-institutional structures whose primary responsibility is to govern. Many prominent scholars agree that an institution has to be capable of mixed functionalities in order to achieve recognition as a state. They have defined the state in a variety of ways agreeing on the core factors that give meaning to statehood. Primarily, two factors determine the extent to which the state could hold claim to legitimacy: Effectiveness in governance and the suitability of the ideological foundation based on which it governs to the core ethical values that the society upholds.

How does the state prove itself effective? It has to overcome a variety of hurdles (economic, social, political and cultural) in order to govern successfully. Certainly, the level at which it could achieve success depends upon its ability to protect and serve the public. Therefore, one of the main criteria for gaining legitimacy is to demonstrate competence through, in John Lock's words, "the preservation of society"[1] which essentially means protecting the lives and liberties of the public.

However, policy execution by itself does not necessarily mean that the public would recognize the state as a legitimate body. The state would need to base its policies and subsequent actions on an ideological foundation at least parallel, if not identical to that of the norms and values of the society. This implies that in formulating and implementing policy, the state would have to consider the public's collective moral identity. Of course, it is likely that some people may or may not morally accept the state's actions. Nevertheless, the idea is not to meet everyone's value expectations, but to form policy that is sensitive to the public's moral values as a whole, and to act in the interest of the society in accordance with the public's shared moral values. When the state takes action consistent with the communal norms and values, it gains the moral authority needed to rule, meeting the public's standard of appropriate governance. This chapter will focus on discussions concerning the state and state legitimacy by scholars such as Max Weber, Joel Migdal, Ashraf Ghani, John Schar, Henri Claessen, Robert Jackson and Carl Rosberg. They agree that a legitimate state is one that has won people's approval in action as well as in principle. On these two grounds, I have used

---

[1] See on line: "Of the Extent of the Legislative Power" <u>Second Treatise of Civil Government by John Locke</u> Digitized: Dave Gowan, Sec. 134. 1-19. 1690.
<http://oregonstate.edu/instruct/ph1302/texts/locke/locke2nd-a.html>.

the Afghan state as a case study and assessed its capacity of earning the public's approval.

Standards of Statehood

What are the required conditions that determine an institution's recognition as a state? In a paper titled "Closing the Sovereignty Gap: An Approach to State-Building," Ashraf Ghani, Clare Lockhart, and Michael Carnahan argue that a state would have to prove capable of fulfilling certain responsibilities and claiming certain rights.[2] They identify ten key criteria as specific prerequisites to statehood. Covering these milestones would mean that the state has proven competent, and capable to fulfill its duties. As a result, it will be able to exercise control over the territory within the boundaries of its jurisdiction. These conditions reflect the state's scope of competence while implementing policy in order to ensure the continuation of its existence.[3]

1. Legitimate monopoly on the means of violence
2. Administrative control
3. Management of public finances
4. Investment in human capital
5. Delineation of citizenship rights and duties
6. Provision of infrastructure services
7. Formation of the market
8. Management of the state's assets (including the environment, natural resources, and cultural assets)
9. International relations (including entering into international contracts and public borrowing)
10. Rule of law

The systematic study of a functional state and the analytical approach of dividing its tasks into various components have expanded the meaning of statehood. This method covers all key areas of control in order to affirm authority. Hence, it seems unreasonable to exclude any one of the conditions mentioned above from this list. Meanwhile, adding new functions would inevitably lead to the expansion of the already existing conditions. A closer look at each one of these functions could broaden one's understanding of, not only the importance, but also the functionality embedded in the elements that shape the identity of the state as a political institution. Any state unable to meet all of these provisions, functions under a compromised circumstance that undermines its identity. Ghani et al warn that state's inability to perform these tasks would lead to:

---

[2] "Closing the Sovereignty Gap: An Approach to State-Building" is available online at Overseas Development Institute: <http://www.odi.org.uk/publications/opinins/44_sovereignty_gap_july05.pdf>.
[3] See: Ghani, Ashraf. Clare Lockhart, and Michael Carnahan. "Closing the Sovereignty Gap: An Approach to State-Building." Overseas Development Institute. Working Paper 253. (Sep. 2005) 6.

> . . . The creation of contending centers of power, the multiplication of increasingly contradictory and ineffective decision making process, the loss of trust between citizens and state, the de-legitimization of institutions, the disenfranchisement of the citizenry and ultimately, the resort to violence (4).

Using their list of functions could prove helpful in identifying the challenges to the state legitimacy in Afghanistan. According to news reports, and based on the extensive studies conducted by human rights organizations, as well as individual political scientists and institutions, the active participation of warlords in the Afghan political process is one of the major hurdles impeding the formation of a sovereign and legitimate state. Warlords are the primary reason for the paralysis of state institutions to perform most, if not all, of the functions necessary to eliminate the gap between the "de jure" and the "de facto" state.[4] While the state is in constant struggle to fight Taliban's insurgency and terrorism, its structural problems revolve around 1) institutional organization and control, which as discussed in chapter six, is severely undermined by corruption 2) micro-economic management and development, again, hampered by drug trade and 3) the provision of services and tools to guarantee functionality and progress at macro-economic level. The third factor seems directly related or perhaps a consequence of the first two mentioned above. It is also evident that there exists a connection between these issues of paramount importance and warlords' control of political, economic and military power.

The Legitimate State

The state is an institution comprised of sub-institutions fundamentally different from all other forms of social, political and economic structures. The central characteristic of the state, initiated by Max Weber and agreed upon by many within the academic community is its ability to establish dominance within a specific territory through the legitimate use of force. Unsurprisingly, this constitutes the first element in Ghani et al's ten essential criteria necessary for making statehood possible.

While Migdal acknowledges the widespread usage of this phenomenon in defining the state, he also emphasizes "the importance of the efforts about the very essence of how . . . societies are and should be constituted - their norms and rules, regulations and laws and symbols and values" (10 - 11). He believes that the state would have to prove itself worthy of consideration as "the proper authority" for presiding over and resolving matters of political, social, and economic significance among the public (10).

---

[4] Ghani et al argue that "there is a clear gap between the de jure sovereignty that is assumed when, for example, international treaties are signed between 'sovereign' states, and the de facto absent or compromised sovereignty that exists in many of these states"(4).

Other scholars, such as Henri Claessen, agree with Migdal adding that the existence of common convictions and values between the state, as the ruler, and the public as the ruled, would create the kind of legitimacy that the state is in need of in order to establish authority (23). Put simple, the difference between the *state* and the *legitimate* state is rooted in the degree to which the public accepts and believes in the moral authority of the state.

Furthermore, Claessen points out that absolute legitimacy is extremely difficult if not impossible to achieve and measure. Thus, he seems to share Swartz's conviction that "it is better to speak of the degree of legitimacy" rather than treating it as an absolute phenomenon. This depends on the relative proportion between public consent in favor of the state, and the disenchantment among those who view it as illegitimate (24).

Another important point to consider is that the state as a whole does not act in a coherent fashion. Joel Migdal contends: "The state is not a unitary actor," which simply means that a central authority does not uniformly control the state's institutions at all times (8). While one makes a specific commitment to achieve a central policy objective, the others may or may not act accordingly. For example, President Karzai (the executive) has appealed many times to the law enforcement agencies of the state to counter the drug industry.[5] However, in spite of such repeated pleas, many of the corrupt police officers, provincial governors as well as the judges act contrary to his demands. Not only do they refuse to curb, but also actively participate in drug cultivation and trade. Contradictions as such between the state's policy and practice are testimony to its amorphous identity. Put simple, the state is not a whole and coherent unit. Nevertheless, let us remember that the state's failure to act unitarily does not mean that it ceases to exist. A state can be imperfect, illegitimate and incoherent, and yet continue to clasp onto statehood.

While discussing the issue of legitimacy, it is also noteworthy that the nature of state's relationship with the society does not exclusively depend on the implementation of the law through the legitimate use of force. A modern democratic state would have to discover new ways of dealing with various groups that adhere to values different from and even contradictory to that of the state. According to Migdal, as the organization encounters various social groups, "it clashes with, and accommodates to different moral orders" (12). This reality is the reason for which the modern state is obligated to adapt to a variety of unexpected conditions in tune with a diverse set of public demands.

Thus, the state remains flexible in choosing policy directions and objectives. Furthermore, the social and economic dynamics play an imperative role in the law making and goal setting process put forward by the legislative and the executive branches of the government (12). Understanding this complexity, a successful democratic state can quickly adapt to the continuing political, economic and social transformations. This altering capability determines the state's policy direction, and the course of action it could take to effectively deal with the constantly changing

---

[5] See chapter seven: "Economics of Drugs: Impact of Drug Trade on State Legitimacy."

conditions. Confirming Migdal's observation in regards to the state's response to these shifting dynamics, this book will demonstrate that the formulation of the state policy by the Afghan political elite has been a rational approach to the demands by socio-economic forces, and a calculating reaction to shifting political realities in Afghanistan. How, then, warlords' involvement in, and manipulation of the democratic system has influenced the state's ability to grapple with these issues?

Coercion or Persuasion?

A powerful state may be able to impose its authority, yet it may or may not be successful in winning people's approval of its rule. Migdal believes that "the more the state seems all powerful, the more likely are subjects to accept it in their ordinary lives" (14). Nonetheless, ensuring acceptance through the use or threat of force does not necessarily transform the state into a legitimate institution. Acceptance is won by winning the public's hearts and minds, not through the use or show of power. In addition, how is one to define a powerful state? If the term powerful were to indicate effective functionality by the law enforcement agencies, then the public would be forced to abide by the laws of the state, fearing persecution and punishment. However, there is a difference between voluntary acceptance of the state rule by the people, believing that its authority is justified and the acceptance of an "all-powerful" state in the absence of alternatives to express disapproval, rejection and opposition. State power unto itself does not necessarily serve as the ground for approval or acceptance of the state authority among the public. An individual citizen (subject) may not accept or agree to his/her subjugation to the state power, but continue to remain obedient to, and as Thomas Jefferson would put it, "constrained" by its rule simply because he/she has to.[6]

The question then remains open to debate. What are the premises based on which the state could claim legitimacy among the majority, if not all, of the public? The fact that an institution meets the criteria for statehood, and is recognized as one, does not necessarily legitimize its rule. It is also important to realize that to be recognized as a legitimate state, an institution would have to be a state first.

Max Weber describes the state as a "political association" (32). Certainly, the state is political because of its primary function, which is to manage, allocate and distribute resources through legislation, adjudication and enforcement of the law. Having said this, Weber warns that the goals that the state strives to accomplish do not solely determine its success in achieving statehood. The means through which it governs also dictates its nature to a great extent. Therefore, "the state can not be defined in terms of its ends" (32). This pertains to the manner in which it sets and achieves objectives.

What separates it from other organizations is a principal characteristic peculiar only to the state. It is the state and no other institution within and or separate from it that

---

[6] Jefferson, Thomas. "The unanimous Declaration of the thirteen united States of America" July 4, 1776. < http://www.ushistory.org/declaration/document/>.

claims ownership and control of the justifiable use of physical force (33). The critical point in Weber's argument is that the state must not only reserve the *right* to use violence, but it also has to be the *only* authority exclusively enjoying this privilege. Thus, he places great emphasis on the importance of empowering the state in order to assure absolute domination. Weber believes that the survival of the state largely depends on the nature of its relationship with its subjects. "The dominated must obey the authority claimed by the powers that be," Weber asserts (33). Nevertheless, domination by itself does not establish legitimacy. Therefore, the state would have to search for means through which it could gain the public's confidence in its rule, and subsequent approval of its governance. This would ultimately lead to the legitimization of its power.

To achieve legitimacy, the state would have to justify its domination by giving reason to the dominated to obey its rule not as a mere consequence of fear, but because of devotion stemming from a sense of trust and respect for its authority. A paper by John H. Schar, titled "Legitimacy in the Modern State" points out the importance of the "belief or opinion" in the state as the "appropriate" or "morally proper" institution.[7] Following this line of argument, it seems reasonable to conclude that in Afghanistan the domination of warlords within the institutional structure of the state has undermined its efforts to achieve legitimacy grounded on the pillars of respect and trust.

Weber mentions three distinct manners in which the state could claim legitimacy: traditional, charismatic, and legal. Traditional and charismatic leadership seem equally important in the state legitimacy discourse. Nevertheless, legitimacy is the focus of discussion in this book. How could the state legally assert domination so that the public conforms to its rule while recognizing the legitimacy of its institutions?

Legal legitimacy is based on a specific element. The state's power would have to be considered morally justifiable among the public. This implies that the state would have to govern according to the norms, rules and moral standards generally acceptable to the majority of the people. State's conduct and the manner in which it handles the day to day business of governance has to take place within a legal framework aligned with public's collective moral standards. Weber refers to this phenomenon as "competence based on rationally created rules" (34). Agreeing with Weber, Claessen also mentions that the state could attain legitimacy through "the conviction that rulers and ruled have a number of norms and values in common" (23). It is sound morality, as the public defines it, which establishes the degree to which a state could lay claim to legitimacy. Keeping collective morality in mind while making policy or acting upon it helps shield the state from moral criticism, and reinforce the suitability of its rule in the public's perception.

Therefore, defining legitimacy from this point of view has little or nothing to do with the use of force or monopoly on violence. To assert legitimacy, the state has to operate according to the principles that make sense and are agreeable to the public.

---

7 Schar, John H., "Legitimacy in the Modern State." Ed. William Connolly Legitimacy and the State New York: New York UP, 1984. 104-133.

Until now, the Afghan state has not been successful in accomplishing this goal while handling the issues of past war crimes (chapter four), illegal drug trade (chapter seven), and institutional corruption (chapter six). This failure, in turn, has proven detrimental to the effectiveness of the state as well as the formation of a positive perception of its rule among the Afghans.

When there appears a rift, or occurs a collision between the guidelines that the state follows in making policy and taking action to implement them, and the collective social morality, the public views the state unrepresentative of its ideals. Henceforth, unable to respect and trust the state, it subsequently perceives it as illicit.

Monopoly on Violence

The use of force comes into play when effective governance becomes the focal point of dialogue surrounding legitimacy. Therefore, it is imperative to study the ability of the Afghan state monopolizing violence while assessing the degree to which it can assert legitimacy. Attempting to serve and protect the public and or its own interests, the state would certainly need to establish this sort of monopoly. In fact, its ability to govern is dependent upon its aptitude not only to convince the public of the rightfulness of its decisions and actions, but also to compel them to follow the rules that they would otherwise refuse to obey. Furthermore, the second element of legitimacy is the ability of the state to prove competent, not simply in governance, but also in serving and protecting its citizens. The Afghan state has simply not been able to exhibit such competence, which has lead to its inability to attain a high degree of legitimacy.

Nevertheless, it is also possible that holding a monopoly on the use of force, the state could continue to survive, and simultaneously disregard fulfilling its obligations to the public. In situations as such, its citizens could hardly regard it as a legitimate institution. This is because one of the factors that legitimize the state rule is the degree to which it serves and protects the public. Through display of power, the state conveys to the people that it remains the supreme authority within the territory under its jurisdiction. This exercise of power helps the state fulfill its obligations to the public. It also helps enhance its image as a feared, but not necessarily respectful and trustworthy institution appropriate to rule. As Robert H. Jackson, and Carl G. Rosberg maintain, "the monopoly over the use of violence gives the state the capacity to exercise control" and "the ability to pronounce, implement, and enforce commands, laws, policies and regulations" (264). Indeed, effective use of force does strengthen the state's ability to govern. However, its capacity to perform the functions mentioned above does not necessarily translate into the legitimization of its rule.

Hence, what makes force/violence the instrument through which the state could attain legitimacy is not the mere use of it, but its *legitimate* use in achieving this end. Following a similar line of argument, Claessen maintains that coercion is legitimate when it is used to reinforce "a number of norms and values" shared between those who rule and those who conform (23). Therefore, the extent to which the state is capable of substantiating itself worthy of governance in both principle and practice determines its success level in asserting a legitimate identity. To claim legitimacy, the state has to "persuade members of its own appropriateness," says John H. Schar (109). Unjustifiable use of force cannot serve as an effective tool to convince the public of just and proper rule. Nonetheless, the demonstration of power consistent with agreed principles between the state and the public could serve as a persuasive device to invoke favorable perception of the state rule.

Conclusion

It is important to distinguish between the definitions of the two concepts seemingly similar, but essentially different from each other – the *state* and its *legitimacy*. This is because the goal of this study is to evaluate the impact of warlords' influence on the legitimacy of the state, and not on its identity (statehood). Ashraf Ghani et al set clear perimeters surrounding the definition of this political unit called the state. The top element in their comprehensive list of ten items is what other scholars, such as Max Weber, have also identified as key factor in separating the state, as a political body from all other forms of institutions. This factor is the monopoly on the legitimate use of violence, which is a criterion of immense importance, arming the state with the authority to formulate and implement policy. This sort of monopoly provides the state with the means necessary to gain and maintain legitimacy.

However, the capacity to use force *alone* does not readily translate into legitimacy. In an effort to prove legitimate, the state would have to engender a belief among the public that it, and only it, is the suitable power deserving to govern, serve, and protect the people in return for obedience and cooperation. The state, therefore, would need to demonstrate *functional effectiveness*, as well as *moral justification* for its rule. These are the two main elements that give meaning to the concept of legitimacy.

Accordingly, it is safe to conclude that the legitimacy of the state depends not only on its ability to serve with competence, but also on the public's perception of its authority. Regarding to the effectiveness and legitimacy of the state rule, the public has two main concerns: 1- Are state's actions and principles morally sound? 2- Is it eager and capable to act in the best interest of the public? Thus, the state can achieve legitimacy if it earns the right *and* demonstrates the will and power to govern effectively. It is with this definition strictly under consideration that this book intends to evaluate the state's degree of legitimacy within the contemporary political and economic realities of Afghanistan.

CHAPTER THREE

The Struggle to Assert Legitimacy

During a chilly afternoon, my family and I huddled on a bench watching a show of magic and juggle by the waterfront. Our bemused eyes remained fixed on the stage witnessing the juggler perform every seemingly impossible trick skillfully and with perfection. Although, the show was free of charge, the unwritten rule was that if the juggler managed to perform all or most of his tricks successfully, meeting our expectation to be entertained, we would voluntarily toss a dollar or two into his hat that conspicuously sat on the left corner of the stage. On the other hand, if the juggler failed to deliver a successful performance, making mistakes such as dropping one of the blazing sticks, or falling off the unicycle while juggling them, we would feel much less obligated to donate our money. Naturally, we would have no reason to clap or cheer for him. We would even feel justified to express our discontent with his performance by booing him off the stage.

Fortunately, our skilled juggler managed to demonstrate impeccable talent and skill. Therefore, throughout his performance we continued to tolerate the chilly wind slapping our faces from every possible direction. In addition, to show our appreciation of his successful performance, we pulled our frozen hands out of our pockets and wholeheartedly clapped and cheered throughout the show. As the performance ended, we voluntarily opened our wallets, and transferred a few dollars into the juggler's hat circling among the audience.

The juggler's struggle to keep the three flying dragon-sticks under control reminded me of the Afghan state. Much like his actions, it also struggles to manage three of the most formidable tasks in such manner as to avoid endangering its own survival, and maintain its credibility intact. While the state has committed itself to waging a war against terrorism, it has continuously struggled to prevent the cultivation of poppy across the country, and eliminate drug's illegal trade. In the meantime, it has found itself obligated to fulfill its promise of reconstruction and gradual economic development to the people of Afghanistan.

However, it is important to mention that for the Afghan state the responsibility of performing these tasks seems much more formidable than that of our performer's. The later has to focus primarily on keeping the balance among the flying dragons while simultaneously maintaining control of a seemingly rebellious unicycle. In this case, the juggler is in control of the situation. The former, on the other hand, has to *fight* terrorism, *eliminate* drugs and *rebuild* Afghanistan while trying to maintain its focus proportionally divided among all three processes at once. The success of these operations would most likely lead to the public's satisfaction as well as a boosted level of trust and respect for, and willingness to cooperate with the state. Just as we expressed our appreciation of the entertainer's winning performance with applause and voluntary financial rewards, the state's success in encountering enormous difficulties such as drugs, terrorism and reconstruction would win people's approval and support that, subsequently, could initiate the recognition of its legitimacy among them. However, unlike our juggler, the Afghan state is not in full control of many factors[8] that impinge on its performance in governing effectively and making an effort to assert legitimacy.

In order to achieve these goals, in addition to formulating sound policies, the state would need to utilize the expertise of loyal and honest government officials to serve, and lead various institutions through effective course of action. To what extent has it been successful in attaining this objective? The leniency of the state's policy in regards to the involvement of warlords in politics has lead to their virtual control of the *Wolosi Jirga*, (the lower house of the parliament) and many prominent military and civilian posts in the government.[9] Subsequently, decelerating the political, social and economic reconstruction of Afghanistan, this strategy has directly contradicted measures taken by the Afghan state and the international community to wage other wars on drugs, crime and corruption.[10]

Hence, this book contends that warlords' success in capturing key positions within the government's newly formed institutions has undermined the legitimacy of the state. It addresses and seeks answer to questions such as these: How has warlords' active participation in the democratic process affected the Afghans' perception of the state? What factors have contributed to warlords' success in holding high-ranking political positions? How do they affect the state's ability to address issues such as corruption, and combating the illegal drug economy? Finally, how do warlords' influence the process of state formation and institutional effectiveness in serving the common interests of the public? While searching for answers to these questions, it is easy to find a great number of empirical evidence that clearly link warlords to drugs, corruption, as well as current and past human rights violations.[11] It is also clear that the public is mostly aware of their history of actions, and present realm of activities. Past war crimes, and current human rights abuses are among the most serious accusations that warlords face. Currently, as corrupt politician with murky histories, they serve in influential public offices representing the state, which is why the public perceives the state itself as corrupt, ineffectual and illegitimate.[12]

As discussed in chapter six, statistics reveal that warlords are in control of a high percentage of wealth through the illegal trade of drugs. In addition, by means of

---

[8] For instance, foreign interventions and socio-political fragmentation.

[9] See chapter four: "Joya and Warlords: Past Crimes and Afghanistan's Future."

[10] Chapter six discusses the political ramifications of drugs on state formation, and chapter seven focuses on the impact of drug cultivation and trade on the economy.

[11] See chapter four, six and seven.

[12] See "Economic and Social Rights in Afghanistan: May 2006: Summary Report." Also see "A Call for Justice: A National Consultation on Past Human Rights Violations in Afghanistan."

political influence, they have added a new dimension to their ability to accumulate wealth and sustain power. Warlords enjoy protection not only through control of important public offices, but also from their own private military forces that number in tens of thousands. As a result, they are able to challenge the authority of the state. The ramifications of their involvement in the Afghan democratic system are beyond violation of justice. Their simultaneous participation in the illegal drug cultivation and trade, as well as the policymaking process and implementation of laws, impairs state's ability to meet people's expectations of improving the quality, and guaranty the security of their lives. While many of its agents continue to pose serious threat to people's liberties and security, the state has failed to prove effective in serving the public. Warlords defy the authority of the state through challenging the basic principles of democratic governance, and imposing their own brand of laws in order to further their agenda at the cost of public interests.[13]

Evidently, studies conducted by reputable human rights organizations, such as the Afghan Independent Human Rights Commission (AIHRC), demonstrate that the public views the state unworthy of its trust and respect.[14] The report concludes that in general "there is a profound lack of trust in government, holders of public office, and to some extent in the international community, as having failed to do anything" addressing the abuses of the past (41). Subsequently, incapacity on part of the state coupled with a deep sense of distrust on part of the public has proven decisive in state's failure to assert a high degree of legitimacy.

What is Legitimacy?

Legitimacy may embody different meanings and values as perceived by various scholars, politicians, and the public. It is therefore important to define this concept in order to avoid subjective usage of it as much as possible while conveying a point or making an argument. To identify a general definition for legitimacy, one could refer to a reputable English language dictionary. The other method is to determine the necessary conditions based on which a state could affirm legitimacy.

Applying the first scheme, a clear and precise definition of the term in focus is readily accessible. The Miriam-Webster dictionary defines legitimacy as "conforming to recognized principles or accepted rules and standards."[15] According to this description, a legitimate state implements laws that it legislates, not only among its citizens, but also within its institutions and among government officials (the agents of the state). This means that the state follows the same guidelines and abides by the same principles that it applies to its citizens. In other words, the state protects its authority from its own threat by keeping public institutions and public servants obedient to the supremacy of its rule. Therefore, the capacity and the will to prevent the violation of political,

---

[13] See chapter six on the impact of corruption and drug on Afghanistan's political economy.

[14] See Introduction to chapter five of "A Call for Justice," a thorough report prepared by the AIHRC on past human rights violations in Afghanistan. Pg. 41.

[15] See: <http://www.m-w.com/cgi-bin/dictionary?va=legitimacy/>.

economic and social rights of its subjects serve as one of the underlying factors in the recognition of the state as a legitimate entity.

Why is it important for the state to ensure and protect its legitimacy? Establishing clear boundaries around powers and responsibilities of the state could prove helpful in assessing its capacity to successfully implement policy, and uphold the rule of law unaffected by outside influences. As it remains free of danger by any external threat, the state stands a better prospect in fulfilling its obligations towards its citizens. In the absence of consideration for personal and or foreign interests, it focuses on making and implementing policies with concerns only concentrated around the interests of the public. Taking the interests of a person or a specific group into account could harm the image of the state as a trustworthy entity. Thus, it is probably safe to assume that under similar conditions, a legitimate state is more likely to serve its citizens efficiently than an illegitimate one.

This partially explains why the citizens of any country would prefer to receive services and protection by a legitimate state. They demand that by giving precedence to their interests, the state remain loyal only to its constituents and not to any other party. Therefore, citizens in general oppose any action or policy that compromises state's allegiance and commitment to the public. This is how the populace seeks to protect its welfare. In addition, when a state manages to keep its credibility intact, it earns the trust and respect of its citizens. This trust and respect reflects the perception of the state in the eyes of its citizens as a legitimate unit. It also seems realistic to expect the public believing in state legitimacy to offer cooperation in implementing the rule of law. Therefore, legitimacy could readily increase state power, not only in public's perception, but also in practice by facilitating the transformation of policy into action.

One of the decisive factors in recognizing the credibility of the state is the extent to which it is able and or willing to take the lead in conforming to the guidelines and abiding by the same principles that it expects the public to follow. If the state's agents fail to value and act upon the rules and regulations that are of its own creation, its attempts to implement those laws could easily prove futile. Hence, the public could begin to doubt its legitimacy when the state refuses to accept accountability.

Moreover, a genuine effort on part of its officials and institutions in creating a transparent political environment could help preserve the legitimate identity of the state. Failure to do so could easily result in the erosion of people's trust in the capacity of the state to serve the public, and protect the citizens' rights and interests. In specific terms, as grounds for subsequent cooperation between the state and its subjects, honesty and fairness are two of the crucial factors affecting peoples' belief in state authority.

Legitimacy is a pillar reinforced by people's confidence in the supremacy of state's rule. Its recognition as a sovereign and legitimate body is of immense political significance. Therefore, it is probably safe to assume that a state that inspires confidence among its citizens, and wins their support is much more likely to remain stable and be triumphant in serving the public than one that cannot earn these privileges.

State Formation

It is critical to consider the role of the illegal drug industry while analyzing the issue of warlords' impact on state formation. Warlords are primarily responsible for managing the drug economy and ensuring the continuation and efficiency of its operations. Their deep involvement in drug trade, as well as their ability to maintain a tight grip on political power, offsets the state's efforts to curb drugs and corruption and affirm legitimacy among the public. This is a manifestation of the state's contradictory policies in regards to warlords' participation in politics on one hand, and drug eradication campaign on the other.

Since warlords are active participants in drugs cultivation and trafficking, their involvement in politics inhibits state's efforts to eliminate drugs. As chapter seven demonstrates, warlords' hold on political power, coupled with strong private military forces, allows them to protect their illegal economic interests from serious threat by the state. Additionally, as principal beneficiaries of the drug economy, the sum of their military, political and economic might is far greater than that of the state. This superiority of power has enabled them to preserve their monopoly on the right to violence, a right supposedly reserved only by and for the state.

Using their weapons, and political position, not only do they intimidate the local population into cooperation, but also provide those who do cooperate with security and livelihood. Enormous wealth created through drug trade helps warlords to fund their private armies adequately. Furthermore, it enables them to bribe government officials such as police chiefs, governors and judges in order to avoid prosecution by the state. In addition, they use their official privileges combined with ethnic, tribal and sectarian ties to other warlords and corrupt politicians in order to break the same laws that they are expected to protect and implement.[16]

Thanks to a relatively free press environment, allegations of corruption as well as past and present crimes against humanity no longer remain secret to the public. Afghan and international media has continuously published news stories of crimes and corruption committed by public officials since the beginning of the post Taliban era.[17]

Conclusion

The political and economic realities of Afghanistan lead one to infer that warlords' manipulation of state organizations, and taking on the leading role in the drug industry, resulting in institutionalization of crime, has forced the Afghan democratic state to face a dilemma in eradicating drugs and combating corruption simultaneously. This, in turn, has profoundly affected the state's governing capabilities, such as effective administration control, and proper execution of the rule of law. Realizing the

---

[16] See an in depth discussion of these issues in chapter six and seven.

[17] See Chapter six on "Corruption and Drug: A Deadly Combination Weakening the Afghan State."

contradictory nature of state's policies, some doubt as to whether democracy has indeed served the best interests of the people. Among many, especially the underprivileged majority, this doubt has turned into disappointment, anger and resentment against the state. Groups such as the Taliban and Al-Qaeda would certainly not hesitate to take advantage of these unsatisfactory political and economic conditions in Afghanistan.

Is it then possible to trust a state that, while making claims of standing for justice and human rights, rewards those accused of human rights abuses, and involvement in drug trade? Since many of its own high-ranking officials have failed to prove trustworthy violating the same laws that they are elected to protect, the Afghan state's status as a legitimate entity remains highly uncertain.

CHAPTER FOUR

Joya and the Warlords

Past Crimes and Contemporary Politics

> My criticism of all my compatriots is why are they allowing the
> legitimacy and legality of this *Loya Jirga* (Grand Council) to
> come under question with the presence of those felons who
> brought our country to this state? They turned our country into
> the nucleus of national and international wars. I believe that it
> is a mistake to test those already tested. They should be taken
> to national and international courts. If they are forgiven by our
> people, the bare foot Afghan people, our history will never
> forgive them.[18]

The above statement is a segment of a speech delivered by Malalai Joya. At the time twenty-three, she represented Faraah province during a Loya Jirga. Representatives from all around Afghanistan and Afghans abroad attended this council. Following the Bonn agreement,[19] the Jirga was held in Kabul Polytechnic Institute on June 11, 2002 to form a new transitional government in an attempt to make a significant stride toward peace, democracy and stability. By devising this new government, the intention was to create a desirable political environment within which to formulate new social and economic policies. Many hoped that this would guide the country towards reconstruction and prosperity.

However, Joya's famous three-minute speech did not focus on the provisions of establishing a new administration. Instead, she argued that many of those ratifying these outlines did not even deserve to participate in the Jirga – let alone enjoying the privilege of casting their vote concerning the new administration's validity. Suspended from the Afghan parliament in May 2007, she served as the representative to the lower house of

---

[18] See "Joya in Loya Jirga" at: <www.malalaijoya.com>.
[19] On December 5, 2001, various political and military factions of Afghanistan signed this agreement in the presence of the Special Representative of the United Nations' Secretary-General for Afghanistan. The main objective of this agreement was to end the conflict and promote national reconciliation while establishing a provisional arrangement pending the re-establishment of permanent government institutions.
For further information see: < http://www.afghangovernment.com/AfghanAgreementBonn.htm>.

the parliament. Joya continues to insist that the participation of warlords accused of war crimes undermines the state's legitimacy, and is contrary to democratic principles.

In support of Joya's argument, far reaching research by human rights organizations demonstrates that Afghans in general believe that warlords have weakened the authority of the state by hijacking critical positions of power in various public institutions around the country.[20] Therefore, the public finds it difficult to rely on the state to provide them with protection, improve their living conditions and defend their rights to life, liberty and justice.

A Brief History

Following the defeat of the Soviet supported Communist regime, street fights began in early April 1992 as Junbesh forces lead by Abdul Rashid Dostam joined forces with Rabbani-Massoud's Jamiat militia. Subsequently, they attacked their long-term rival, Gulbuddin Hekmatyar's Hezb e Islami. Hezb had already captured the Interior Ministry, and the *Arg* (presidential palace). The battle inside the city continued for three days until Hezb retreated to the southern margins of Kabul. On May 30, the war resumed among the factions. Jamiat and Hezb began firing heavy weaponry such as rockets, and artillery at each other, most of which landed on residential areas and public utility facilities. Meanwhile, in the west of the city, the radical Sunni Ittihad militants lead by Abdul Rab Rasul Sayyaf, and Abdul Ali Mazari's (killed in 1996) Wahdat militia engaged in street battles. They faced each other in the residential areas of Kabul exhibiting utter disregard for the safety and security of the civilians.

It is noteworthy that during these battles, public abduction, torture, rape and murder was not the result of accidental mishap of the crossfire between the enemy combatants. Generally, Afghans believe that these crimes were intentional acts of gross human rights abuses fueled by ethnic and sectarian hatred as well as the desire for power and domination. As Washington Post reported, while both parties weakened and lost the war, they joined the other two dominant armies of Hezb and Jamiat.[21] As the war continued, hundreds of civilians were murdered, and many became hospitalized, "lacking electricity, water, and basic sterilization equipment."[22] These events occurred almost immediately after the collapse of Najibullah's government.

Mujaheddin or Warlords?

Heads of states, political scientists and the public have given warlords a diverse set of titles. During the Afghan-Soviet war, many called them *Mujaheddin*, (plural for Mujahed) freedom fighters and soldiers of God. It is clear that these titles are of positive

---

[20] See Effects of Bringing War Criminals to justice in "A Call For Justice: A National Consultation on Past Human Rights Violations in Afghanistan." Pg. 17. This report is prepared by AIHRC.
[21] Ittihad joined Jamiat, and Wahdat collaborated with Hezb.
[22] See "Afghan's Faith: Healing or disintegration?" Washington Post

religious and or political connotations. For example, according to the Islamic doctrine, it is the duty of a Mujahed to fight against injustice, corruption and any oppressive force threatening to harm Muslims' interests. However, the Marxist regimes, against which the Mujaheddin fought for more than a decade (1978–1989), in an attempt to demonize the enemy, labeled the various factions of the resistance movement as one homogenous group of *ashraar* (the evils). Followed by the demise of Najibullah's regime, and the advent and continuation of the civil war, (1992-1996) understandably, the public began to refer to these warring factions as *jang-saalaaraan*, (warlords) or *tofang-salaaraan* (gun lords). Nonetheless, during and after the U.S. military attack on Taliban, referring to warlords, some used the newly invented euphemistic titles such as *regional strongmen* and *militia forces* to identify these private militant groups.[23]

In any organization, the existence of corrupt elements is possible, especially during desperate circumstances of war. Therefore, it may not be reasonable to label all men who fought in the past wars as one category – strongmen, Mujaheddin, warlords, ashraar etc. To generalize and assume that any particular group member, leader or commander is representative of a party or a group's collective character is to make hasty conclusion on faulty premises. Therefore, this book identifies *only* private professional armed individuals, whose purpose has been to contend through aggression over control and distribution of resources and power against the state, (including the right to collect taxes and monopolize violence) as warlords.

Joya did not specifically categorize the identity of warlords according to their membership to any particular group, or the nature of their political belief and objective. She insisted on the identification and prosecution of those accused of war crimes according to their history of human rights abuses rather than political affiliations. Warlords with "blood stained hands" do not exclusively belong to any one specific political party or military faction.[24] Nevertheless, with the help of the human rights organizations, it is easy to identify many of the high ranking, as well as mid-tier commanders that Joya has alluded to as war criminals. However, during her speech she did not make any mention of a specific person or group. Perhaps she refrained from doing so for the fear of potential danger to the safety of her life.[25]

Testimonies and Evidence

Whatever the reason, the lack of adequate evidence and or witnesses to testify in support of her claims could certainly not have been the only reason for speaking in

---

[23] See articles published by the <u>USA today</u> - "U.S., coalition forces battle rebel forces in Afghanistan," published at:http://www.usatoday.com/news/world/2003-01-28-afghanistan-fighting_x.htm; and the <u>New York Times</u> – "Rise in Violence in North Shows Afghanistan's Fragility." <http://www.nytimes.com/2007/05/29/world/asia/29afghan.html?ex=1338091200&en=86deda041c1c243a&ei=5088&partner=rssnyt&emc=rss make references to warlords as strongmen and militia forces>.

[24] This is the title of a report prepared by HRW: "Blood Stained Hands: Past Atrocities in Kabul and Afghanistan's Legacy of Impunity."

[25] See <www.malalaijoya.com> for listening to a full clip of her speech during the Loya Jirga.

general terms. Extensive reports prepared and published by organizations such as Human Rights Watch (HRW), the Afghan Justice Project (AJP), and the Afghanistan Independent Human Rights Commission (AIHRC) serve as supporting evidence to Joya's allegations. These studies suggest that warlords' participation in the state's various institutions (judiciary, legislative, law enforcement) has greatly undermined its credibility in the eyes of the Afghan public. For example, HRW provides a detailed account of the war crimes committed by warlords from 1992 to 1996, illustrating that the public views these private military groups responsible for human rights abuses.

Established in 1978, in an effort to identify and support the victims of violence, this organization's main objective is to investigate and report human rights violations. It insists on accountability on part of the violators through regular and systematic investigation. HRW is not only active in Afghanistan. It covers human rights issues in South America, the Middle East, and Asia. During the three decades of its operations, HRW claims to have remained free of ties to any government or political party. It also asserts that its report of the April 1992 – March 1993 street battles of Kabul is largely free of political subjectivity. The report discusses in detail, and provides numerous eyewitness accounts as to how military factions terrorized the civilian population while fighting to seize control of the city.

The Unforgotten Past

In spite of tremendous efforts by humanitarian organizations in collecting statistical data from this period, there still exists no exact number of all lives lost during this war. However, estimates show that these battles lead to at least 50,000 civilian deaths. (1992-1996)[26]. Confined to only a district or neighborhood, as each militia group fought to expand its territory, "streams of blood ran through the city," said an eyewitness.[27] According to the HRW report, a summary of the different ways in which warlords committed crimes as follows:

> . . . indiscriminate military attacks, [on civilians], intentional targeting of civilians, murder and assaults on civilians, abductions, forced labor, looting of civilian homes [and] raping of women as well as girls and boys (4).

It is important to realize that these are not mere accusations, but the end results of 150 interviews, based on individual experiences of actual events, reported by residents of Kabul. Who should be held responsible for these criminal acts? HRW lists the names of groups it finds accountable for the crimes summarized in this study.

---

[26] Karon, Tony. "Afghanistan: One Gun, One Vote" Wednesday, Nov. 14, 2001
<http://www.time.com/time/columnist/karon/article/0,9565,184593,00.html/>
[27] Author's interview with a Kabul resident.

The Responsible Parties

As shown below, the factions and leaders involved in the documented abuses include:

- *Jamiat-e Islami-yi Afghanistan* (hereafter "Jamiat"), a predominantly Tajik faction led politically by Burhanuddin Rabbani and commanded militarily by Ahmad Shah Massoud (killed in a suicide attack on September 9, 2001).
- *Shura-e Nezaar,* a federation of military forces led by various Mujaheddin commanders, mostly from the north and northeast of Afghanistan, united under Massoud's military command.
- *Hezb-e Islami,* a predominantly Pashtun faction under the command of Gulbuddin Hekmatyar, and one of the primary recipients of military assistance from the United States and Pakistan through the 1980s and early 1990s.
- *Ittihad-i Islami Bara-yi Azaadi Afghanistan* (hereafter "Wahdat"), the principal Shi's and predominantly Hazara faction in Afghanistan led in 1992-1993 by Abdul Ali Mazaari (killed in 1996) and heavily supported by Iran.
- *Junbesh-e Milli-yi Islami-yi Afghanistan* (hereafter "Junbish"), a predominantly Uzbek and Turkmen militia, based in northern Afghanistan, led by Abdul Rashid Dostam (a general in the Soviet-backed Afghan army during the 1980s) and comprised of forces from the former Soviet-backed army and various Mujaheddin militias from the north of the country.
- *Harakat-e Islami-yi Afghanistan* (hereafter "Harakat"), a predominantly Shi'a faction headed politically by Mohammad Asef Mohseni and militarily by Hussein Anwari, supported by Iran.

Source: "Blood Stained Hands: Past Atrocities in Kabul and Afghanistan's Legacy of Impunity." <u>Human Rights Watch</u> Pg 5. (2005).

HRW holds the political and military leadership of each faction mentioned above mainly responsible for the crimes committed either as a result of their own direct orders or, indirectly, through actions taken by their subordinates. This is because each group had organized based on vertical chains of command, effectively allowing the commanders to manage, lead, and remain fully aware of their operational logistics:

> Each of these forces in 1992-1993 had hierarchical military structures, with a chief commander, sub commanders at various levels, and soldiers. These hierarchies made it possible for functional leaders and commanders to have effective control over subordinates (6).

This statement clearly focuses on one point – the organizational structure of armed groups had enabled the commanders at various levels to remain in control of their forces. Subsequently, the report continues to argue that group responsibility principally lies on the shoulders of the leadership. Effectively, it makes a preemptive effort in countering the argument that the leadership is not to be blamed for atrocities committed by the subordinates because they had lost full command of their forces.

Whatever the case may be, the realities of the bloody battles of Kabul are yet to be disentangled from myth in the formal sitting of a national or international court. It appears that the people of Afghanistan have not forgotten the bitter memories of those wars, including the pain of loosing their loved ones. A vast majority of the population continues to demand justice, and ask for help from the international community to assist the current administration in fulfilling what they seem to perceive as an obligation. Indeed, a survey conducted by Afghanistan Independent Human Rights Commission (AIHRC) in 2005 authenticates this point.

According to this study, more than 94 percent[28] of the Afghans consider justice for past crimes to be important or very important (75). In addition, more than three quarter of Afghans (76.4%) think that bringing war criminals to justice will "increase stability and bring security" to Afghanistan. This number is considerably greater than the 7.6% of the population contending that the prosecution of war criminals would lead to political instability and subsequent threat to national security.[29]

Aside from the emotional aspects of this issue, the logic behind such strong resolve to prosecute war criminals is based upon two main premises. First, the active pursuit of justice is more likely to dissuade, if not entirely prevent, other private militant forces from committing similar crimes. Witnessing armed men roam freely in villages and small towns is a major cause for concern among the people. After all, the public has experienced more than two decades of war's horrors and destruction. Therefore, it is not surprising to discover that 1530 of 1800 Afghans interviewed by the AIHRC declared that security was their "most serious concern"(16).

Secondly, the demand for prosecution of war criminals is illustrative of the Afghans' key expectation from democracy – establishing a fair political system with the highest regards for accountability and respect for the rule of law. The public argues that without proof of innocence, none of the suspects and those accused of crimes should be given the opportunity to participate in the political process. People expect the system to deliver many promises, among which one is social and political justice. Thus, a well thought strategy for the removal of criminal elements from the state institutions could serve as an instrument with which it is possible to build a more stable and legitimate state.

The desire for justice and accountability is well depicted in opinions expressed by many ordinary Afghan citizens. In an interview with AIHRC, a woman from Kandahaar emphasized the importance of a trustworthy leadership: "We need the kind of leadership that can gain people's respect" (15). Similarly, a resident of Daykhundi argued that "genuine implementation of law and having law abiding citizens will

---

[28] 75.9% of the Afghan population believes that justice is very important, and 18.5% sees it as important, which add up to 94.4%.

[29] See "Effects of Bringing War Criminals to justice in" A Call For Justice: A National Consultation on Past Human Rights Violations in Afghanistan Pg. 17. This report is prepared by AIHRC.

guarantee justice" (14). It is difficult to argue that people with high regards for law and justice are likely to have faith in the legitimacy of a state lead by individuals believed to be war criminals.

What type of crimes are warlords accused of exactly, and what kind of test have they not been able to pass according to the public? Does the severity of these crimes justify risking political stability by placing them on trial? Attempting to find answers to these and many other questions, the HRW report has interviewed thousands of ordinary citizens, many journalists, and experts on Afghan politics, documenting widespread war crimes committed by major militant factions. The results clearly indicate that war criminals have grossly violated the human rights and liberties of a vast number of innocent civilians in every imaginable manner. If not dealt with lawfully by the state, warlords are likely to repeat the same crimes over and again. Subsequently, realizing that the state, with a weak grip on the administrative control[30] is not the supreme authority, the public will continue to lose confidence in the legitimacy of the state.

Once the state proves incapable of adequate management of crime, it looses the right and privilege to govern. The protection of its citizens' life and liberties are among the most vital conditions, based on which the state could assert legitimacy. Of course, to achieve this, it would have to insure control over the means of violence. In other words, it would have to prove to its citizens that it is the state, and no other party in charge of law making and law enforcement. It would also need to communicate clearly to the public that it holds everyone, including its own agents and institutions, equally responsible for deference to the laws of the state. The Afghans find it difficult to count on politician-warlords, sharing a not too distant history of war crimes and human rights abuses, with the control of key public offices and scarce economic resources. Since warlords are in command of many of the prominent positions in various state institutions, the populace is unable to rely on these institutions for the protection of their basic human rights. Put simple, the public views the state as unfit to rule.

Ittihaad

HRW claims that Ittihaad's forces have murdered a vast number of people, including women and children, during the Kabul battles. This claim is based on several interviews with west Kabul's surviving residents. One civilian described how innocent people were caught in the crossfire between the heavily armed fighting factions:

> I could see the women and men rushing away from the fighting, running down the street towards us. At the same time, some of the bullets or shrapnel from the explosions were hitting people. So men and women were falling down in to the street (25).

---

[30] See chapter three: Ghani et al's list of key prerequisites for statehood.

This eyewitness account is testimony to the display of absolute disrespect for civilian lives as Ittihaad and Wahdat fought against each other. Apparently, the meaning of their names (unity), which in itself exemplifies a paradox, is not the only shared attribute between the two. The story of a man who, in spite of being a Pashtun, was kidnapped and jailed by Ittihaad's militants serves as another vivid example of human rights violations committed by this group.[31] This man was arrested because of a personal dispute with one of the group members. He told HRW of his horrifying experience while in captivity sharing a cell with thirty to forty Hazara[32] prisoners:

> I could hear these people, Sayyaf's people, talking about retreating. And at one point, one of them said to commander Torgul, 'What should we do with these prisoners?' . . . Somebody said, 'go and shoot them.' When I heard this, I hurried away and hid away from the door in the corner of the room. A person came, and shot all over the room. About ten people were killed immediately, and four were wounded. We were trembling with fear (48).

Murder of innocent civilians is not the only crime that Afghans accuse Ittihaad and other militant groups of committing. These warlords also kidnapped civilians subjecting them to torture and abuse, simply because they belonged or appeared to belong, to a certain ethnic or religious group. Subsequently, thousands were murdered, and those who did survive continue to live with serious emotional and physical scars of the past. A hospital employee described the heart wrenching physical and psychological conditions of the abducted victims of torture who somehow had managed to survive and made it to the hospital:

> I saw what they had done to them – people beaten up, people who had been tortured. They had put RPGs [Rocket Propelled Grenades] in to the anus. They gang raped girls. I saw these victims (49).

People of Kabul had not fallen victim to merely one group's atrocities. Virtually all parties involved in street battles had subjected individuals and groups of people to brutal acts of violence.

Following the intense fighting among Mujaheddin factions, in February 1993, the Rabbani-Massoud government in cooperation with Ittihaad's forces planned and executed attacks on Kabul's Afshaar district, where Hezb and Wahdat had established their headquarters. Subsequently, they looted an estimated number of 5000 households. According to HRW, there is credible and consistent evidence of widespread and systematic human rights abuses encompassing violations of international humanitarian law during and after these operations (74). Additionally, residential areas were fired

---

[31] Ittihaad's membership is predominantly comprised of the Pashtun ethnic group.

[32] An ethnic minority group who mostly adheres to Shiat sect of Islam.

upon by BM-22, BM-40, BM-12, and Sakr-18, 105 mm canons, 82 mm and 120 mm mortars. The organization interviewed many of the Afshaar's residents to investigate the nature of these offenses. During one of these interviews, a resident described the mayhem that lead to the destruction of his home:

> They were firing at the top of the hill. I remember I heard my son shriek. I was wounded also, in the torso here in the stomach. My grand daughter was also killed by the same shell, and my other daughter was wounded in the face and disfigured. My house was on fire (75).

After reading and hearing of stories as such, it becomes clear that people's demand for prosecution of war criminals does not seem unreasonable altogether. HRW report mentions the names of the following Ittihaad commanders allegedly responsible for crimes similar to the one briefly described above. Abdul Rabb al Rasul Sayyaf, Zalmai Tofaan, Mullah Taj Mohammad, Abdullah Wardak, Jaglan Naeem, Abdul Manan Diwana, Noor Aqi, Amanullah Kochi, Mushtaq Lalai, Shirin, Mullah Kachkol.[33]

Wahdat

Similar to other militia groups, many Afghans hold Wahdat responsible for murder, rape, kidnapping and torture of civilians. Racial and sectarian hatred as well as the desire for dominance seem to have been the driving force behind committing these heinous crimes. A journalist reported that Wahdat's forces lead by Abdul Karim Khalili, abducted Pashtun civilians assuming no or little distinction between Ittihaad's militiamen and ordinary civilians who happened to resemble members of a certain racial group or religious sect. HRW has presented a brief description of the way Wahdat's men treated their prisoners:

> They pulled out the fingernails of prisoners, cut off hands, cut off legs, and even hammered nails into prisoners' skulls. Humans were kept in containers and containers were set on fire (4).

Many of the abducted men and women disappeared forever. Those who did survive will have to live with their physical and psychological wounds, inflicted by warlords of Wahdat and other militants, for the rest of their lives. Malalai Joya claims that these are the victims on behalf of whom she demands justice from the Afghan government and the international community. HRW insists that among the Wahdat's leadership in command Abdul Karim Khalili, Abdul Wahid Turkmani, Mohsin Sultani,

---

[33] See HRW report, as well as pages 112 and 114.

Tahir Tofan, Sedaqat Jahori, Commander Bahrami, Shafi Dewana, and Nasir Dewana need to be held responsible for committing war crimes.[34]

Hezb e Islami

The most serious crime that people accuse Hezb of committing is the indiscriminate assault on Kabul with rockets and other heavy weapons (1992-1994). Hezb has been known as the long-term rival and enemy of Jamiat. The two parties' elites have been extremely successful in recruiting and mobilizing supporters through the promotion of ethnic and linguistic polarization (Pashtun vs. Tajik) among the Afghans. Furthermore, the intrusion of foreign governments, particularly Afghanistan's neighbors, has reinforced the continuation of a hateful relationship between the two.[35]

In April 1992, after Massoud and Dostam's forces pushed Hezb to the southern margins of the city, Hekmatyar established a military base there firing an abundant number of heavy weapons at the city's residential and commercial districts. Hezb argued that its objective was to damage the government owned radio station, the airport and the presidential palace. However, to many residents of Kabul it appeared that Hezb's men attempted to aim at any thing *but* those targets.

Subsequently, thousands of civilians were murdered and entire neighborhoods reduced to ashes and dust. Resulting in great devastation, the attacks were lethal. Emphasizing their destructive impact, the HRW describes them as "the most deadly attacks of the period" (29). Finally, Hekmatyar failed to capture the city. Nevertheless, he did succeed in shredding scores of children into pieces in front of their parents' eyes. A woman described to HRW's researchers what had happened after just *one* of the rockets had hit in her neighborhood:

> [My neighbor's] son had been sitting near this wall outside, where the artillery landed, and he was completely blown up. This woman here was running about, collecting pieces of [his] flesh in her apron, and crying. Her son's name was Sakhi. He was completely blown up - disappeared. Her grandson, Mukhtar was also killed in the same explosion (30).

There are many stories as such published in the HRW report. However, these are a few examples of the horrors that the residents of Kabul had to experience. This is to understand why many of the Afghans express unhappiness and frustration with the state's current policy concerning warlords. The stories mentioned in this chapter paint tragic pictures of the horrific crimes inflicted upon innocent civilians as the immediate results of warlords' cruel abuse of power. It is therefore easy to note that the horrendous experiences of yesterday, coupled with the political realities of today, are of great

---

[34] See HRW report, as well as pages 111 and 110.

[35] Author's observation through five years of living in the midst of these rivalries in Pakistan.

significance in shaping the Afghans' perception of not only the newly elected government, but also democracy as a whole.

HRW finds Hezb e Islami's leadership, comprised of Gulbuddin Hekmatyar, Commander Sabawon, Kashmir Khan, Toran Khalil, Toran Amanullah, Commander Zadran, Engineer Zulmai, Nurul Rahman Panjshiri, General Wali Shah and many others responsible for war crimes and human rights violations in Afghanistan.[36]

Jamiat

Witnesses have testified that during the 1992-1993 wars, as well as the Afshaar operations in 1993, Jamiat's leadership and armed forces fired numerous rockets into the residential areas, leading to civilian deaths in and around the city. Positioning themselves in strategic locations around Kabul, such as the Mamorin Mountain, Jamiat's combatants had "intentionally [fired] rockets into occupied civilian homes" (36). In the words of a civilian "they would target any thing that moved" (37). Other than random shooting of civilians, HRW has recorded accounts of "pillage and looting" perpetrated by Massoud's men as they captured the city. On July 8, 2003, an Afghan journalist described to HRW the indiscriminate acts of violence by Jamiat's militia as those of the "animals doing whatever they wanted" (53). In an environment of absolute chaos and horror, "you'd notice blocks getting hit. Roof beams were torn out of the houses, electricity wires torn out," said another witness (55). Many blame commander Massoud, whom later (September 9, 2001) was assassinated by two Arab men disguised as journalists, in part responsible for the murder of Kabul's civilians and destruction of the city. According to HRW, in addition to Massoud, Mohammad Qasim Fahim, Bismellah Khan, Gul Haidar, Younis Qanooni, Baba Jan, Abdul Momin, Basir Salangi, Kabir Andarabi, Haji Almas, Baz Muhammad Ahmadi, Mullah Ezzat, Baba Jalandar, and Ahmadi Takhari are among many of the commanders accountable for the atrocities committed during these operations.[37]

Junbesh e Melli

Similar to other private militia forces involved in the Kabul street battles, Junbesh's men, to whom Afghans refer as "Gelam Jam,"[38] also committed pillage, kidnapping, rape, and murder. The HRW report substantiates this claim through making reference to a statement by one of Junbesh's own high-ranking officials. He has even pinpointed some of the commanders involved in these criminal acts:

> Shir Arab, Ismail Diwanah [crazy] and Abdul Cherik from the
> beginning engaged in widespread looting of the market . . .

---

[36] See HRW report, as well as pages 116 and 119.

[37] See HRW report, and pages 119-120.

38 It literally means rug collector. When Junbesh's men looted people's houses, they made sure that the household was stripped off all of its belongings, including the rug underneath their feet.

> They looted the Porzaferoshi Bazar . . . Ismail Diwana was in
> Bala Hessar [south-east of Kabul]. He regularly killed and
> robbed Pashtuns from Paktia who were passing through on the
> way to Kabul (56).

Following extensive research, AJP has also prepared a detailed report of war crimes by virtually all parties involved in the 1994 conflicts. Interestingly, the organization points out that the information it has gathered and presented constitutes only a fraction of the human rights violations during the resent history of Afghanistan (5). This means that the scope of these crimes is of far greater magnitude than what has been uncovered and reported until now. The study, published in 168 pages, estimates that 2500 civilian lives were lost as the battles continued from January to June of that year. Importantly, the report holds Hezb and Junbesh mainly accountable for this tragedy. This time though, these parties did not fight against each other. Instead, united they attacked Jamiat, which at the time claimed to have seized control of the city. According to HRW, some of the Junbesh commanders who have taken active part in committing these crimes are Abdul Rashid Dostam, Abdul Cherik, Majid Rouzi, Mohsin Homayun Fauzi, Jura Beig, Rasul Pahlawan, Zeini Pahlawan, Rahim Pahlawan, Shir Arab, and Ismail Dewana.[39]

History of Crimes and Violence

One of the most important points that AJP emphasizes is that the occurrences of crimes against humanity did not begin with street battles among warlords after the demise of the Marxist regime. The frequent human rights abuses have been a continuous trend since 1978 when the cold war was ignited on the Afghan soil. Among the accused perpetrators are not only the warlords. AJP indicates that the former Marxist governments of Taraki, Amin, Karmal and Najib as well as the Taliban have committed their share of human rights violations and war crimes (4). The international humanitarian organizations insist that many members of these groups, but not all, share a long history of crimes against humanity in Afghanistan.

However, they warn that the classification of all members of these parties as one (war criminals) would be a mistake. For example, AJP clearly states that it does not assume that "every single fighter has been guilty of such actions" (4). Additionally, the organization argues that it is an "independent research and advocacy" group, whose intention is *not* to defame or attack the credibility of any particular party or individual, but to "document war crimes and crimes against humanity" (1).

It is also noteworthy that humanitarian organizations involved in fact finding efforts on human rights issues claim that the targeting of residential areas and downtown Kabul with artillery and rockets has not been the result of an accident or technical failure. They believe that those weapons were "aimable and accurate,"

---

[39] See HRW report, and pages 121-122.

suggesting that the attack on Kabul was a deliberate attempt to create an atmosphere of terror and chaos in order to exhibit military might (HRW 39). Perhaps haunted by fear of rebellion and defeat, warlords' objective was to weaken people's spirit and discourage a possible public uprising. This line of argument is based on testimonies given by Kabul residents and evidence implying that the commanding authorities deliberately planned and executed the killing of civilians based on the racial and sectarian affiliation of the victims (profiling), and not because of their involvement in armed conflict.

Assessing Accountability

According to the international laws of combat and the international law for the protection of human rights, the responsibility of decision-making carries great importance leading to serious consequences for those in command during a war. This responsibility is divided into two main categories - *direct* and *imputed* command.[40]

The first, direct responsibility, applies when the commander/leader orders his/her forces to act against the international human rights laws. The law of direct command interprets this crime as if the commander him/herself has committed the offense(s) directly. It says that even if the crime has not taken place but been ordered by the commander, the commander would still be held responsible and remain subject to punishment for initiating the order (HRW 108).

The second type of leadership accountability, namely the imputed command responsibility finds the decision-making authority responsible for all crimes, whether ordered or not, committed by any of the individual subordinates. A superior who is capable of preventing a crime from occurrence by his/her forces, but does not exercise this power, is considered equally guilty of that crime as the perpetrator directly involved in committing it (HRW 109). The Yugoslavia and Rwanda's war crimes tribunals, established by the United Nations in 2003, have seriously considered this principle while conducting investigations and prosecuting war criminals.

Considering these definitions of command responsibility, it is difficult to argue that in Afghanistan commanders must not be held responsible because they were unaware of the crimes that their subordinates had committed. Within more than two decades of war, the scope of war crimes has been widespread and horrific in nature. This vivid reality makes it extremely difficult for the leaders to claim ignorance of the terror and chaos that their forces had spread throughout the city.

---

[40] According to HRW, "the culpability of superior officers for atrocities that their subordinates commit is commonly known as command responsibility. Although the concept originated in military law, it now also embraces the responsibility of civil authorities for the abuses committed by persons under their direct authority." For more information, see "Command Responsibility." <http://www.hrw.org/press/2001/07/chain-of-command.htm>.

According to the in-depth research, and numerous news stories from Afghanistan, the nature of relationship between the militants' leadership and their subordinates seems to have been clear. To a great extent, the commanders maintained control and command of their subordinates most of the time. This fact increases the likelihood of proving them guilty in the court of law. Collected data provides plenty of evidence[41] that confirms the application of both (direct and imputed) definitions of command responsibility to war crimes committed by either commanders or their subordinates in Afghanistan. It is therefore easy to claim that those in command have repeatedly violated article (3) of the Geneva Convention,[42] which has been ratified not once, but four times. In 1956, Afghanistan was one of the signatories to this article. Thus, one could maintain that it fully applies to war crimes in this country since that time period (HRW 101).

International humanitarian law also defines a particular set of crimes as "crimes against humanity [that] outrage the conscious of human kind" (HRW 102). During the

---

[41] Examples of which has been previously presented in this chapter.

[42] Article 3 of Geneva Convention states:

"In the case of armed conflict not of an international character occurring in the territory of one of the High Contracting Parties, each Party to the conflict shall be bound to apply, as a minimum, the following provisions:

(1) Persons taking no active part in the hostilities, including members of armed forces who have laid down their arms and those placed ' hors de combat ' by sickness, wounds, detention, or any other cause, shall in all circumstances be treated humanely, without any adverse distinction founded on race, colour, religion or faith, sex, birth or wealth, or any other similar criteria.
To this end, the following acts are and shall remain prohibited at any time and in any place whatsoever with respect to the above-mentioned persons:

(a) violence to life and person, in particular murder of all kinds, mutilation, cruel treatment and torture;

(b) taking of hostages;

(c) outrages upon personal dignity, in particular humiliating and degrading treatment;

(d) the passing of sentences and the carrying out of executions without previous judgment pronounced by a regularly constituted court, affording all the judicial guarantees which are recognized as indispensable by civilized peoples.

(2) The wounded and sick shall be collected and cared for.
An impartial humanitarian body, such as the International Committee of the Red Cross, may offer its services to the Parties to the conflict.
The Parties to the conflict should further endeavour to bring into force, by means of special agreements, all or part of the other provisions of the present Convention.
The application of the preceding provisions shall not affect the legal status of the Parties to the conflict."
Source: International Humanitarian Law: Treaties and Documents. <http://www.icrc.org>.

Nuremberg tribunal, the international criminal court used this legal phenomenon to specify crimes that had inflicted physical and mental injury to defenseless civilians because of systematic, planned and intentional attacks by the warring military forces.

Moreover, to protect non-combatant civilians from crimes against humanity, which are more likely to take place in wartime, article 51 (2) of additional protocol to the Geneva conventions plainly states: "'The civilian population as well as individual civilians, shall not be the object of attack'" (HRW 103). This law applies to all sorts of military conflicts at local, national and international levels. Its objective is to protect civilians and the facilities where there exists a great concentration of civilian population, such as schools and hospitals, from violence. Taking into consideration the definition of crimes against humanity, numerous testimonies by Afghan civilians suggest that warlords have committed violations that could be classified as war crimes according to the international law. The bitter memories of war crimes do not help warlords earn the privilege of serving the very same public that they are accused of terrorizing not too long ago.

Afghans Demand Justice

AJP and HRW's reports reflect the views that the Afghans generally share concerning the warlords. People do not trust them, among many, for two main reasons. Firstly, they believe that warlords have already failed to create a peaceful and just political environment in which the society could flourish. Henceforth, they argue that Afghanistan can no longer afford to take the risk of failing again by allowing the warlords to rule. Secondly, they find warlords' continuous involvement in drug trafficking, institutional corruption and violence reasonable cause for concern. Their long-standing historical record of inaptitude in governance, and disregard for the rule of law has resulted in the loss of faith in warlords among the general public.

Warlords have continued to maintain a strong grip on their informal bases of political, military, and economic power. Many have even succeeded in further strengthening their authority within the current political system. Research shows that this has initiated the loss of public's trust in the legitimacy of the political process as well as in the ability of the state to protect the interests of the people. A Call for Justice, a report published in 2004 by the Afghanistan Independent Human Rights Commission (AIHRC) has concluded that there exists "a profound lack of trust in government" (41). Warlords possess the capability to not only participate, but also control and manipulate the institutional makeup of the government, and subsequently, the implementation process of policy as to further their own interests.

For Afghans, what makes an alternative system to the current arrangement possible is justice. In fact, more than 90% of men and women interviewed by the AIHRC said that the government should remove human rights abusers from their posts (77). This number is a strong indication of the publics' desire for action against the warlords. Since many of the accused are employed by the state, this would mean a step toward widespread institutional reform and reorganization. The state, however, seems incapable and or unwilling to take such a risk, fearing political destabilization and the resurgence of militant resistance nationwide.

Why do Afghans demand justice? Among many, one important reason is to ensure that their need for security is met. Once the state brings to justice those who have committed crimes, they will no longer be free and capable of subjecting the civilian population to similar atrocities again. In addition, the service of justice could help deter those who are likely to break the law from committing crime should the opportunity present itself. Many believe that one of the ways through which the state could guarantee civilians' security is to take strong measures against war criminals, and effectively deal with the issue of past crimes. A statement by HRW precisely reflects this point: ". . . so long as those responsible for past crimes enjoy impunity, the security of ordinary citizens is at risk" (4). Certainly, the concern for security ranks high on the public's list of expectations from the state.

Based on the soaring demand for security and great stipulation for justice, AIHRC has titled its report A Call for Justice - a call, which unfortunately is yet to be answered. In other words, the government has not taken specific steps to draft an effective strategy challenging warlords' authority, nor has it successfully implemented provisions for their arrest and prosecution.

AIHRC was established in accordance to the article (6) of the Bonn[43] Agreement signed by major political players in 2002. The agreement had declared the creation of such entity indispensable to research, collect and publish facts pertaining to the past and present human rights violations in Afghanistan. Hamed Karzai, views the existence of this "truth seeking" institution crucial to empower the people (AIHRC 5). His statement is a precise reflection of people's desire for living in a fair and equitable society free of fear from warlords.

As a step towards achieving this goal, the organization conducted extensive interviews with 4151 civilians from January to August 2004. It gathered data while documenting respondents' individual and collective opinions on the issues relating to war crimes and human rights abuses. Furthermore, to ensure the quality of their study, they gathered an additional number of 2000 participants divided between 200 focus groups. AIHRC then documented respondents' individual and collective opinions on the issues relating to the human rights violations of the past (55). The researchers asked questions about topics such as the importance of seeking truth, the meaning and significance of justice, and the role of governmental and non-governmental institutions in addressing human rights matters. They also asked questions about the need for judicial process, vetting, reparation, and reconciliation.

---

[43] This agreement served as a foundation for the establishment of an interim government after the fall of the Taliban.

A careful analysis of the findings from this study suggests that more than three quarters of the afghan population, regardless of their ethnic, religious or linguistic affiliations, overwhelmingly demand accountability on the part of the state (17). The report conclusively deduces that a vast majority of the Afghans is in favor of prosecution of and fair trials for war criminals.

How do the public views justice? Although accountability is the central theme of its definition, they attribute a much broader and multifaceted meaning to this notion. The majority of those interviewed see "the upholding of basic human rights including the freedom of expression, the freedom to participate in elections, the elimination of discrimination on the basis of race, language, and gender . . . the promotion of economy, [and] rule of law" strongly associated with justice. (AHIRC 14). In other words, for the Afghans justice entails a much broader connotation than simply punishing war criminals.

Meanwhile, among a list of top twelve living priorities, the public voted for restoring security as the most important necessity in Afghanistan (16). Clearly, security plays a fundamental role in creating the conditions needed to make peace, and maintain a stable environment for the feasibility of social and economic development. Research, such as that of the AJP's, on human rights issues firmly argue: "An essential part of the process of establishing legitimate administration in Afghanistan is the removal of war criminals from positions of authority" (8). This is not a view held only by the organized human rights communities. Most Afghans as individual citizens also see a connection between security and justice. In fact, 76.4% of those interviewed insist that prosecution of war criminals would ensure security in Afghanistan. On the contrary, less than 8% of the population believes that seeking justice for the victims of war crimes would undermine stability and security (17). It is important to note that those in favor of taking action against warlords constitute a clear majority among those interviewed. As evident, they do not believe that seeking justice would lead to negative consequences of serious magnitude for the state.

The gap between the majorities, who feel security is related to, or even dependent on justice, and the few who disagree is wide. This indicates widespread support for justice among the Afghans hoping to establish a peaceful living environment. Thus, it is not surprising to observe that there exists a "distinct desire" for institutional reform within the state organizational structure among a vast number of the population (15). It is also clear that the state has not only failed to bring those accused of crimes to justice, but it has in fact rewarded them with higher political and economic standings. This has granted the warlords the opportunity to use state institutions and operational systems against its own authority. The public, however, wishes to see those guilty of crimes and corruption stripped off their endowed powers and privileges. Therefore, allowing warlords to participate in the new political process and providing them with new economic opportunities seems not only unfair, but also unsafe for the long-term political stability and equitable economic development of Afghanistan.

The results that the current democratic structure has produced have give rise to a sense of disappointment and despondency among the Afghans in general. As with any other nation, they rightfully demand that the state protect their lives and liberties. But warlords and corrupt government officials involved in illegal drug trade have clearly rendered the state incapable of effectively offering this service to its citizens. Observing widespread corruption among government's various institutions, people feel betrayed and even victimized by the very system that is supposed to ensure justice and equal opportunity for all.[44] A woman interviewed by AIHRC expressed her frustration over the infiltration of corrupt elements in the government's organization. She voiced her concern about the lack of opportunity for effective leaders to ascend, and serve the public: "We need the kind of leadership that can gain people's respect. We do have good people in Afghanistan, but unfortunately these gun lords do not let good people work" (15). Reflecting the results of research by organizations such as AIHRC, AJP, and HRW, her statement serves as an example of the public's general perception about the state. It also raises an important question. Without much reason to trust the state, is it possible for the public to respect and recognize it as a legitimate entity?

Trust, Respect and Legitimacy

It is undoubtedly difficult for the state to gain people's respect while allowing warlords and drug dealers to control key positions in the government as either bureaucrats or key policy decision makers. After all, any government's institutional functionality is mostly the product of a network of individuals with various skill levels operating within a specific policy framework. While warlords share the responsibility of serving the public, they also have the power to undermine people's well-being in order to protect their own self-interest. Unfortunately, many with political influence and strong ties to other corrupt officials and warlords have chosen to further their personal economic interests and political power at the expense of the public's right to security and justice.

Witnessing and experiencing corruption, nepotism, and unfair treatment by many government officials, the public is wholly aware of these realities. It is therefore not too shocking to observe that 58% of those interviewed by AIHRC expressed concerns and admitted that they could not trust the judiciary system (22). Particularly, they did not seem pleased about the fact that even the judges had proven to be dishonest. While deciding on a case, the amount of bribe money (in most cases accepted only in the form of U.S. currency) as well as their ethnic, tribal, religious and linguistic ties to a particular group or person play a more important roll on their decision making process than the credibility of witness's testimony or reliability of the evidence.

Many exiled Afghans, who have returned to Afghanistan hoping to reclaim their real property (confiscated by former regimes or warlords), complain about the lack of transparency within the judicial system. Upon their arrival from Afghanistan to the

---

[44] Also, see chapter six: "Corruption and Drugs: A Deadly Combination Weakening the Afghan State."

U.S., as they speak of the new developments in the country, they do mention that scores of women have returned to schools. The reconstruction of new roads and hospitals, the burgeoning of the new publications in every major city is evident, and finally Afghans have been able to elect their president. However, the story that is inevitably responded by shaking heads as a sign of disappointment and disbelief is the tale of the judges whom explicitly demand bribe in cash inside the courthouse.[45]

Based on the conduct of the state's officials, it could only be expected that 72.5% of respondents told AIHRC that if and when the prosecution of the individuals accused of war crimes takes place, they prefer the international community, and especially, representatives from the United Nations to either observe or take active part in the trial process (25). This study indicates that most Afghans demand supervision of war tribunals by the international community due to concerns about the unfair adjudication of the law by the current judiciary system.

Would it have been possible to obtain similar results, had the entire population been asked the same question? Although it is difficult to predict the answer, statistical data compiled by AIHRC strongly suggest that the majority of the Afghans desire transparency as well as security and justice in Afghanistan. International human rights organizations have openly stated that nepotism, bribery, and disregard for the laws of the state has created distance between the state and the public.[46] This detachment often manifests itself in the form of frustration, disappointment, and distrust of the government within the society.

Arriving at similar conclusion, AIHRC invites the Afghan authorities to formulate an effective strategy for implementing what it calls "transitional justice" in order to resolve issues surrounding war crimes and the abuses of the past. It argues that devising such strategy is required to regain people's trust in "holders of public office, and to some extent in the international community" as having failed to act promptly tackling the issue of institutional corruption (41). The organization offers this proposal after establishing a clear connection between the ability of the state to operate accountably and the level of trust among the public.

Not only do people view those accused of crimes undeserving of public office, they also demand their prosecution in a national or an international court. Studies indicate that most Afghans presume that the state and the international community are responsible for the structural reform of the government institutions. In 2004 for example, when researchers asked a randomly selected number of individuals from all of the thirty-two provinces of Afghanistan as to when should those accused of crimes against humanity be placed on trials, 44.9% said "now" and 25.5% voted for a two to five years delay (AIHRC 20). According to this survey, presently (2008) 71.4% of the sampled population expects the state to take immediate action against warlords.

---

[45] Based on the writer's numerous interviews with Afghans who have traveled to Afghanistan during the 2002-2007 periods.

[46] See Delesues, Lorenzo and Torabi Yama. "Reconstruction National Integrity Survey: Afghanistan 2007." The National Integrity System
<http://www.tiri.org/dmdocuments/RNISS%20Afghanistan.pdf>.

Subsequently, it is unsurprising to discover that 61% of those interviewed oppose nationwide amnesty for the war criminals (AIHRC 22). With respect to the demand for justice by such a large number of the population, ignoring this issue could by far be viewed as insult to the innocent civilians who have fallen victim to the grave human rights abuses of the past.

Recent news and reports from Afghanistan are illustrative of a system in which warlords, by taking advantage of high-ranking positions in government institutions, serve as the principal force behind the survival and operation of the illegal drug economy.[47] Many liable for legislation and implementation of the law have repeatedly broken it themselves. Indeed, within the state organization, there are several officials suspected of, as HRW phrases it, staining their hands with the blood of innocent Afghans and engaging in other unlawful activities – i.e. drug trade. If it were reasonable to believe that the leading authorities of the state are corrupt and guilty of crimes, it would not be reasonable to expect the public to respect and trust the institutions that officials as such manage and control. Clearly, government's apparent inability to seek justice for the victims of the past war crimes and its unwillingness to address the issue of widespread corruption related to drugs has rendered its efforts fruitless in asserting complete legitimacy.

Conclusion

It is important not to assume guilt on part of those accused of crimes. However, it is equally important to note that an overwhelming amount of evidence strongly suggest that many of the warlords are guilty of crimes and human rights violations. For this reason, not only Malalai Joya, but also a substantial number of the Afghan population demand that the accused be relieved of their responsibilities, stripped off their powers, and placed on trial. For those who deny accountability for misconduct, this will provide an opportunity to prove that they are innocent. Moreover, it could fulfill the public's most serious demand for improved security conditions nationwide.

On political grounds, as demonstrated in this chapter, statistical data as well as the results of discussions with focus groups gathered from around the country, clearly demonstrate that the level of trust and respect for the state is extremely low among the public. This means that people in general have difficulty recognizing the sovereignty and believing in the legitimacy of the state. Taking this reality into account, the absence of serious institutional reform plays an important role in shaping people's perception of the state authority. The state has failed to win the Afghans' hearts and minds through resolving issues such as the fair and effective implementation of law, security establishment, curtailing corruption, and eradicating drugs. These issues constitute the underlying factors contributing to delay in the creation of a stable political environment, and the formation of a capable state. In other words, through engaging in and sustaining illegal activities, warlords prevent democracy's promises to materialize, and even

---

[47] The issue of warlords' impact on the drug economy is discussed in chapters six and seven.

jeopardize the very existence of the state. As discussed in chapters six and seven, a complex and interwoven network between warlords, corrupt government officials and drug traffickers (often one agent playing all three roles simultaneously) have distorted the image and undermined the effectiveness of the state.

However, it is encouraging to realize that the possibility to curtail the involvement of militants and those accused of past and present crimes by bringing them to justice is real. The results of extensive surveys conducted by organizations such as HRW, AIHRC and AJP show that the state has a solid case against the militant groups such as Ittihaad, Jamiat, Wahdat, Hezb and Junbesh. The next question is this: To what extent is the state capable of disarming warlords, neutralizing their authority and ending their participation in the new political process? Chapter five will explain the rationale for which the state hesitates to conduct serious institutional reform in order to seek justice for the victims of violence, eliminate official corruption and wage an effective war on drugs. As studies imply, its inability to embark upon these issues of serious consequences has lead Afghans to believe that the state has not earned the kind of admiration that a legitimate body would deserve.

CHAPTER FIVE

Reconciliation and Appeasement

Why Are the Taliban and Warlords Able to Participate in Afghanistan's Democratic Process?

The parliamentary and provincial elections held on September 18, 2005 were among the first organized since the decade of constitutional monarchy (1963-1973) in Afghanistan. As a result, 249 members were elected to represent the Afghans at the *Wolosi Jirga* (the lower house of the parliament).

What is astonishing about this election is that warlords, including four former high-ranking officials of the Taliban's expelled government, comprise at least half of the house's membership. As discussed in chapter two, international human rights groups have accused most of these men of drug production and trafficking, as well as committing atrocities against the people of Afghanistan. Civilians claim to have fallen victim to, or witnessed crimes committed by them since as early as the beginning of the Afghans' resistance against the Soviet invasion (Kolhatkar and Ingals 1). Ann Jones, the author of Life without Peace in Afghanistan writes that at a minimum 17 members of the lower house are "narcotic traffickers," and 40 command their own private armed groups. She also categorizes 24 members as "criminal gangs," and points out that another 19 are accused war criminals alleged to have committed human rights abuses (4). Analysts have raised serious questions as to whether many members of parliament actually deserve the high profile positions, which they have managed to secure.

Why the current administration has allowed warlords and Taliban to participate in the recent parliamentary elections? The newly established state organized these elections with the economic and political support of the international community lead by the United States. Therefore, it seems appropriate to study the Afghan government's guiding principles, as well as the shared perception among many of the U.S. policy makers in regards to the role of warlords and former members of the Taliban leadership in the current political process. The Taliban elite as well as warlords have succeeded to participate in the current political process primarily because the U.S. backed Afghan state has chosen to undertake the policy of reconciliation and appeasement in dealing with them. Based on careful calculations, it has deliberately embraced this policy in an attempt to retain its grip on power at the center. This is due to two main factors.

Firstly, the current administration lacks the economic muscle and the military might to keep warlords and former Taliban elite subordinate to its authority. Second, when the U.S. policy of Afghanistan's democratization comes into conflict with its policy of the war on terror, it seems that for the Bush administration success in the war on terror policy has taken precedence. Many U.S. foreign policy framers have viewed and or treated the Afghan warlords favorably. Since the beginning of the U.S. military operations in Afghanistan, warlords have continued to cooperate with and support the U.S. military in its quest for destroying Al-Qaeda and the Taliban forces.

Who is back in power?

Many did not expect the Afghan government to allow the former leaders of the Taliban administration to participate in parliamentary elections - one of the main cornerstones of democratic process. However, the unexpected indeed has occurred. A total number of six high-ranking Taliban officials run in September 2005 parliamentary and provincial council elections, two of whom were elected in the people's council, *Wolosi Jirga,* of the national assembly.

Mullah Abdul Salam Racketi is one of them. He was the commander of military unit No.1 in Nangarhar province during the Taliban era. Currently, Racketi represents the southern province of Zabul in the parliament. Another prominent Talib participant is Maulawi Mohammad Islam Muhammadi. Muhammadi, who is the former governor of the Bamiyan province (the province in which Taliban destroyed the 157 foot statue of Buddha) during Taliban's era, has secured a seat in lower house on behalf of Samangan province. The Taliban's former foreign minister Mawlawi Wakil Ahmad Mutawakili also had the opportunity to claim candidacy in the western Kandahar province - the power base of the Talib movement. Mutawakili, however, did not win a seat (Radio Free Europe 2005).

One could expect that the significance of the position that these former Taliban leaders had held in the past could easily serve as grounds for holding them accountable for widespread human rights abuses and crimes that the Taliban government is accused of committing. Surprisingly, not only has the government failed to press charges against these men, it has also given them the opportunity to participate in the electoral process, and rise to prominent power-positions within the very administration that forcefully replaced them a few years ago.

Members of the Taliban political elite are not the only individuals whom have enjoyed the opportunity to participate in the recent parliamentary and provincial elections. Many warlords, who belong to various radical and militant political factions, have also taken great advantage of the current political process. They too have participated in the recent parliamentary elections. Furthermore, President Karzai has appointed some of the most prominent leaders of private armed groups as police chiefs, provincial governors and army commanders.

In addition to international human rights organizations, a large number of Afghan civilians hold many of these former Mujaheddin and militia commanders responsible for the physical destruction of the country. They also hold warlords accountable for killing, and various human rights abuses of the innocent civilian population. Therefore, the public is despondent with the state's policy of appeasement toward former cooperating Taliban elites and the warlords. Abdul Rab Rasul Sayyaf, Abdul Rashid Dostam, Fahim Qasim, and Hazrat Ali are a few prominent examples among hundreds of powerful warlords whom have been able to penetrate into the various branches of the government.

This political development has lead to the public's disappointment in general, and the international humanitarian organizations' despondency in particular. They expect the new administration, backed by a community of pro-democracy, pro-justice nations to prosecute war criminals, or at least, acknowledge responsibility on their part. The desire for justice is evident among Afghans, "I will never accept or forgive the people who killed my son," says the seventy-six years old Aminullah. Rebel fighters killed his teenage son accusing him of espionage for a rival faction (Chu 1). "If I could face Karzai, see what I would tell him," he added believing that the state has not fulfilled its duty of protecting the lives and liberties of its citizens (Chu 1). The rift between government's actions, or lack thereof, and the principles that the state claims to have based those actions on appears as a manifestation of hypocrisy. This mismatch between the values that the public anticipates the state to respect while formulating and implementing policy, and the actual path that it follows, leads to the Afghans' perception of the state as incapable and untrustworthy. Individuals affected by war crimes, view the state's responsibility to prosecute war criminals primarily as a moral obligation.

Similarly, proponents of human rights believe that the state is also compelled by law to bring the violators of human rights to justice: "The state has a legal obligation to investigate, prosecute or extradite individual perpetrators of serious crimes," insists Aleem Siddique, a spokesperson for the U.N. Assistance Mission in Afghanistan. He finds it crucial for the Afghan state to take the necessary measures in resolving the issue of past war crimes committed by warlords, which would not only ensure justice, but also add to the state's credibility in the eyes of the public.

Furthermore, this legal obligation essentially pertains to the three of the most important criteria that Ghani et al deem vital for building an effective state.[48] Rightful monopoly on the means of violence, administrative control, and rule of law are among the key factors that enable the state to protect its citizens, take measures to prevent crime, and prosecute those who commit it. Undoubtedly, such capabilities would give credence to the state's rule as a sovereign body. However, warlords' success in penetrating the various governmental institutions demonstrates the state's limitation in securing all three key legitimizing elements. Unable to meet these conditions, it has subsequently failed to prosecute war criminals. This serves as one of the main factors contributing to its incapacity in achieving full legitimacy.

---

[48] See chapter three: Statehood and Legitimacy.

Abdul Rab Rasul Sayyaf

Sayyaf is a dedicated follower of the puritanical Wahabi[49] sect of Islam with origins rooted in Saudi Arabia. In addition to securing a seat in the lower house of the parliament, he was also one of the finalists running for the House Speaker position. Similar to many other Afghan Islamic parties, Sayyaf's *Ittihaad-e Islami Bara-yi Azadi e Afghanistan* (Islamic Union for the Liberation of Afghanistan) party has been greatly successful in using religion as a political instrument not only to gain support among the Muslim population of Afghanistan, but also to solicit financial and military aid from Saudi Arabia.

Interestingly, following the 9/11 attacks on World Trade Center, the U.S. government initiated contact with him hoping to gain his support on the ground during the U.S. air strikes on Taliban. It did so by sending a group of CIA agents to Afghanistan via Central Asia. This team, called the Jawbreaker, was principally responsible for contacting the afghan anti-Taliban warlords in order to ensure their political support and military collaboration. By handing out at least three million dollars (a miniscule amount by today's standards of warfare budget) to warlords who opposed the Taliban regime, it succeeded in buying their support of, and loyalty to the U.S. military operations in Afghanistan.[50] The U.S. political elite have focused intensely and almost solely on achieving the much-desired goal of destroying the Taliban and Al-Qaeda forces. In the meantime, as evidence suggest they have failed to take into account the future ramifications of unwavering military and economic support to warlords.[51]

Based on this platform, Sayyaf was one of the first prominent warlords approached by the CIA. Gary Schroen, author of the <u>First In: An Insider's Account of How the CIA Spearheaded the War on Terror in Afghanistan</u>, explains in his book how he asked Sayyaf for cooperating with the U.S. forces in the war against the Taliban and Al-Qaeda. Sayyaf's participation in these operations, as a Pashtun commander, was of special military and political significance for the United States. During their first meeting, in return for the money that Schroen had given him, Sayyaf had pledged to assist the U.S. forces in their quest to topple the Taliban regime. Schroen writes in detail about Sayyaf's reaction to his $100,000 offer:

> I produced a $100.000.00 bundle of cash from my backpack and handed it across the table to Sayyaf, who instinctively took the package. . . Unlike the money I had passed to the Northern Alliance, I had left this bundle in its original clear plastic wrapping so that Sayyaf could see what it was. Sayyaf held the bundle for a second or two, looking at it, seeming somewhat confused by what he was holding in his hand. . . 'This is the

---

[49] "Wahabism is among the most conservative forms of Islam." John L. Esposito, <u>What Everyone Needs to Know About Islam</u>, p.50

[50] Woodward, Bob. "CIA Led Way With Cash Handouts." <u>Washington Post</u> November 18, 2002 < http://www.washingtonpost.com/wp-dyn/articles/A3105-2002Nov17.html>.

[51] See discussion on the "U.S. Foreign Policy" in this chapter.

first time I have ever accepted cash directly from anyone.' He
shook his head as if he had been tricked, eyeing me carefully, a
slight smile on his lips (117).

The important point to note about this story is that a hundred thousand dollars
has effectively influenced on a warlords' decision to shift drastically loyalties from one
extreme to the other. Therefore, it is surprising to learn that the U.S. places its trust in
the hands of Sayyaf, whose character appears highly amorphous and unpredictable.
Sayyaf had accepted Schroen's offer promising to fight against Bin Laden - a man with
whom he had fostered a close relationship during the years of Jihad against the Afghan
Marxist regime. Most likely, sharing a strong belief in the Wahabi radical religious
doctrine has played a constructive roll in fostering this friendship.

After the Sudanese government's extradition, in May 1996, Bin Laden accepted
Sayyaf's invitation to return to Afghanistan.[52] Upon Laden's arrival, Sayyaf received
him as a guest. One could argue that the U.S. could easily hold Sayyaf responsible for
cooperating with and assisting Al-Qaeda in the past. Later on, his decision to stand
against the Taliban and Al-Qaeda, not only has discouraged any attempt of pressing
charges against him for the alleged war crimes of the past, but has also won him power
and prestige.

Abdul Rashid Dostam

With over 10,000 private militiamen, some believe that Dostam serves as the greatest
military challenge to the newly established and under-equipped national army of
Afghanistan.[53] His forces are highly experienced in warfare, and adequately equipped to
travel through, and fight in the country's harsh terrain. Similar to many other warlords,
Dostam generates revenues primarily through illegal public taxation, and drug trade.
However, what separates him, as a skillful political opportunist, from other warlords is
his unpredictable and deceitful nature. Within the past two decades, his actions have
clearly demonstrated his ability to adapt to an ever-changing political environment.

When deemed appropriate, Dostam has forged alliances with, *and* fought against
most major political parties since his rise to power as a self proclaimed general in the
late 1980s (Schroen 357). Political parties such as Jamiat, Hezb, Ittihad, Wahdat, and
former Marxist regimes of Babrak Karmal, and Najibullah were ironically among his
best allies and worst enemies, depending on the outcome of a political transformation in
a particular time. As reward for his cooperation with the U.S. military forces, President
Karzai appointed him as the special envoy to the north in 2002. Dostam was also one of
the candidates for presidency in 2004. In March 2005, the president appointed Dostam
as advisor to the Ministry of Defense – a position with nominal prestige rather than real

---

[52]See <http://en.wikipedia.org/wiki/Osama_bin_Laden>. under the subtitle: Refuge in
Afghanistan.

[53] For more information on Dostam and other Afghan warlords, see the online journal
<http://ariaye.com>. published mainly in Dari.

value in terms of power and responsibility (Duparcq 1). Some perceive his recent appointment as a positive step toward sidelining Dostam in particular, and warlords in general.

Nonetheless, the international humanitarian organizations and many Afghans have demanded that Dostam be placed on trial for allegedly committing war crimes. Considering the seriousness of this stipulation, Dostam seems to have been successful in not only avoiding trouble with the law but also protecting his space on the national political arena. This is not astounding because he continues to secure tremendous military and economic might reinforcing his bargaining position with the state.

Fahim Qasim

Fahim inherited the command and leadership of Northern Alliance[54] following the assassination of Ahmad Shah Massoud on September 9, 2001. Throughout the 1992-1993 battles of Kabul, as a second tier commander, Fahim was in charge of a group of militants in *Cart e Mamorin*. He used this strategic location as a watchtower over vast areas of the city, from where he could easily target and shoot the enemy. However, HRW reports that based on statements by eyewitness civilians and journalists, Fahim's men practiced target shooting on innocent individuals either walking or riding a bicycle in the streets of Kabul (37). During the Afshaar operations (Feb/1993), he served as one of the Jamiat's prominent commanders supposedly aiming to disarm Wahdat's militants. Human Rights Watch calls it "the most integrated use of military power by the Islamic State of Afghanistan," during which thousands of civilians lost their lives, or were kidnapped, tortured and rapped by Massoud's Jamiat, and Sayyaf's Ittihad forces (71).

After the defeat of the Taliban and the establishment of a new interim administration, Fahim served as Defense Minister in the transitional government. Afterward, President Karzai relinquished him of his responsibility. In July 2004, as he announced his candidacy for the presidential elections, the president dropped Fahim's nomination for vice presidency as well, and replaced him with Ahmad Zia Massoud. Since then, Fahim has refused to disarm his private army, and transfer his allegedly

---

[54] Northern Alliance (United Islamic Front) is a loose coalition among anti-Taliban forces located in northern provinces of Afghanistan The UIF was comprised of roughly five of the factions of Mujahideen fighters:

- Islamic Party of Afghanistan - *Jamiat-I Islami-yi Afghanistan* - Made up of mainly Persian-speaking Tajiks, led by Burhanuddin Rabbani.
- Islamic Unity Party of Afghanistan - *Hizb-I Wahdat-I Islami-yi Afghanistan* - Made up of Shia Hazaras, once led by Abdul Ali Mazari, and later by Mohammed Mohaqiq.
- National Islamic Movement of Afghanistan - *Junbish-I Milli-yi Afghanistan* - Made up of Uzbeks and former communists, led by Abdul Rashid Dostum.
- Islamic Movement of Afghanistan - *Harakat-i-Islami-yi Afghanistan* - Shia, led by Ayatollah Muhammad Asif Muhsini.
- Islamic Union for the Liberation of Afghanistan - *Ittihad-I Islami Bara-yi Azadi* - Pashtun, led by Abdul Rasul Sayyaf.

hidden stockpile of weapons from Panjsher to the Afghan National Army in Kabul. Therefore, in spite of his marginalized position on the political stage, his military might remains a serious threat to the stability of the state. Understanding the grave significance of this reality, Karzai has formally recognized his title as Marshal. He has also endowed Fahim with special rights and privileges that distinguish him from other military officers.

Fahim has been accused of unlawful practices and misuse of his official position for his own personal gain at the expense of public's rights and liberties. In a September 2003 U.N. special report on housing and land rights, Miloon Kothari accused him and Yonus Qanoni (the current speaker of the lower house in the parliament) of unlawful confiscation of people's property in Sherpur district of Kabul, and reassigning them to other warlords and government officials.[55] This accusation could have lead to serious consequences for both men. However, the charge was completely disregarded by the Afghan authorities. One could easily interpret the state's treatment of this case as a sign of its weakness relative to personal supremacy of warlords.

Promising to cooperate with the U.S. forces in the war against the Taliban and Al Qaeda, Fahim received considerable support from the C.I.A. This is clearly evident in Gary Schroen's detailed account of his meeting with Fahim and other Northern Alliance commanders, during which Schroen had given him a large sum of money:

> I produced the backpack with the $1 million and explained to Fahim that these funds were to assist in preparing his military forces for the coming battle. I said I had given Aref[56] $500,000 the night before, and hoped those funds would be used primarily to strengthen Aref's organization. I stressed that other money was available if and when specific needs were identified" (101).

The U.S. financial and military backing of warlords certainly is indicative of its *political* support as well. This creates difficulty for the Afghan state, which is highly dependent on the U.S. military and economic aid for challenging the authority of warlords in order to maintain its monopoly on the legitimate means of coercion.

---

[55] To read more about the abuse of power in land grabbing, see: Constable, Pamela. "Land Grab in Kabul Embarrasses Government." Washington Post Sep. 16, 2003. This and other articles relating to the issue of illegal land confiscation are available at: <http://www.hewad.com/news1.htm>.

[56] Engineer Aref was the head of the Northern Alliance intelligence services.

Hazrat Ali

Purportedly linked to drug trafficking and human rights violations, Hazrat Ali is among the winners of the parliamentary elections in the eastern province of Nangarhar (46). Under the current administration, he has served as the police chief of four provinces – Nangarhar, Konar, Noristan, and Laghman. Some attribute his success in elections to a strong tribal base and his ability to spend lavishly the money earned through drug trafficking during his campaign. In regards to the allegations of his ties to drug production and smuggling, Ali insists that he utterly dislikes poppy because Islam prohibits drug's use, and that he would not hesitate to take serious measures within his jurisdiction to curtail it (Baldauf 2). However, farmers in the province tell stories that are contradictory to his claims. They maintain that Ali's men constantly make sure that the farmers continue to cultivate opium (Baldauf 2). News reports as such, and studies published by human rights organizations lead one to believe that Ali is in fact deeply involved in the illegal drug industry.

The United State's support of Fahim, Sayyaf, Dostam, Ali and other warlords neither is a secret, nor is a new foreign policy strategy. During the Cold Ward era, the U.S. espoused radical Islamist parties, including Gulbuddin Hekmatyar's Hezb e Islami. It provided them with economic support and military training necessary to increase their resistance power against the Soviets and the former Marxist regimes in Afghanistan. According to Barnet Rubin, a leading authority in Afghan politics, from 1986 to 1990 the U.S. and other pro-western governments provided $5 billion in military aid to anti-Soviet religious parties.[57] As part of this aid package, Mujaheddin received a large number of heavy weapons such as rockets and artillery. Following the demise of Najibullah's regime, they launched these weapons on Kabul killing thousands of the city's residents.

Reconciliation or Regression to Chaos?

Is political destabilization of the state and endangering the life, liberty and security of the Afghans a price worth paying to guarantee warlords' cooperation? In spite of the compelling historical evidence exemplifying horrific consequences of military aid to warlords and radical militants, some still believe that in order to defeat Al Qaeda and Taliban it is necessary to provide the warlords with more weapons and other forms (training, financial) of support.

For example, after the unfortunate events of 9/11, in a paper titled "Rebuilding Afghanistan: Fantasy Versus Reality," Lieven and Ottaway[58] argued that the U.S. must

---

[57] See The Fragmentation of Afghanistan: State Formation and Collapse in the International System by Barnet Rubin - p. 179.

[58] Marina S. Ottaway is the director of Middle East Program at Carnegie Endowment for International Peace.

Anatol Lieven was a Senior Associate at the Carnegie Endowment in the Global Policy Program. He is a journalist, writer and historian.

cooperate with "regional leaders" to ensure the effectiveness of its operations against the Taliban (6). They insisted that this would prevent warlords from cooperating with the enemies of the United States. One wonders if the authors were fully aware of these "regional leaders'" history of crimes, and human rights abuses. Whatever the case may be, their argument appears to be based on a narrow view pertaining to the operations of the war on terror, and re-establishment of security and stability in Afghanistan. In fact, regrettable events of the past clearly demonstrate the consistency of grave consequences of the U.S. support of private armies in Afghanistan. Leading to Afghans' rescue from the tyranny of the Taliban, warlords' empowerment has indeed undermined peace, justice, and the democratization process, subjecting this nation to forms of oppression similar to those of the Taliban.

Although somewhat dispersed, the military power of warlords is of great magnitude. According to some estimates, in Afghanistan there exist more than 1800 military groups, encompassing 128,000 armed men. These men have access to more than 15 million weapons of various capabilities (Sedra 13). Undoubtedly, their presence has greatly challenged the state's authority struggling to preserve its territorial sovereignty as well as the security of its citizens. Meanwhile, the capabilities of the inadequately equipped and underpaid Afghan National Army (ANA) clearly fall short of matching those of the warlords.[59] In many of his speeches and interviews, President Karzai has emphasized on the relatively weak position of the state verses the power of the warlords: "Among the threats to the security of our people is the discernable weakness of police presence in our districts, particularly in those areas affected by terrorism, and insecurity" (Sedra 13). Echoed in Karzai's statement, the realities of the state's policing power exemplify serious limitations to its law enforcement capability. He presents a vivid example describing the security situation in various parts of the country: "A typical district in the south of Afghanistan with over 60 thousand population has only an average of 45 policemen" (Sedra 13). The state's position in contrast to political and military domination of the warlords partially explains government's response to their pre-eminence in the Afghan political arena.

Those who believe that the strategy of appeasement represents the state's best option hope and predict that taking this route would discourage warlords from active military resistance against the state. They argue that strict measures taken against the armed and experienced warlords could easily lead to widespread military confrontation and violence beyond state's ability to contain. In addition, they maintain that in reaction to the state's crackdown policy, many militants could join the ranks of the Taliban and Al Qaeda. This will expose the Afghan population to inter-ethnic animosities that could damage the national unity of the country. Therefore, in the interest of peace and national unity, they insist, reason dictates that compromise with warlords is the best option.

Based on the interpretation of the events that have unfolded since the fall of the Taliban, one point is clear. To compromise with warlords is not only to ignore their crimes of the past, but also to reward them with key positions such as chief of police,

---

[59] See "Afghanistan Security: Efforts to Establish Army and Police Have Made Progress, But Future Plans Need to be Better Defined." United States Government Accountability Office June 2005.

parliamentary membership and ministerial positions in various government institutions. Deciding to act in accordance to this line of reasoning, in Spring of 2004, chair of National Reconciliation Commission, Sibghatullah Mujaddedi as well as President Karzai announced national amnesty inviting opposing and hostile groups to join the government in an effort to create a stable and peaceful environment. Karzai announced this policy hoping to provide warlords and former Taliban members with an opportunity to assimilate within the new democratic system.

Supporting the president's decision, Zalmai Khalilzad, the then U.S. ambassador to Afghanistan asserted, "There must be a place of honor for those who cooperate" (Miller 4). In the light of Afghanistan's current economic condition and military capabilities, and the recent history of war and violence, reconciliation indeed appears a sound policy choice. However, there is need for a clear definition of "a place of honor" as well. Does honoring those who cooperate necessarily mean awarding them with prestigious positions in the key public institutions? Proponents of human rights and a great number of Afghans seem to disagree with the allocation of *any* space for war criminals in public institutions regardless of their level of cooperation. Also, there are other questions still open to debate. What is the acceptable definition of cooperation in this context? How should the state react if a warlord joins forces with the Afghan military to fight against the Taliban and yet continues to harass civilians? Evidence suggests that the unwillingness or the inability of the Afghan state to address these issues is the outcome of strategies such as the war on terror largely beyond its own control.

The weak military and economic position of the state relative to that of the warlords is another reason for its failure to confront the enemy. Thus, the current administration finds no other choice more pragmatic but to compromise. So far, the result has been an increase in warlords' political influence, military might and economic supremacy. Senior commanders are not the only players benefiting from this arrangement. Continually committing various forms of crimes, scores of sub and mid-tier factional commanders have taken full advantage of state's leniency in regards to accountability and discipline.

In particular, their involvement in drug trade has provided them with funds sufficient to launch large-scale military operations. This has posed a serious challenge to the authority of the state. Economic supremacy coupled with a form of complex network founded on tribal, ethnic and sectarian ties with the government officials, has enabled them to maintain and strengthen their mini-fiefdoms at district, city, and even provincial levels. Consequently, they have successfully monopolized the right to exercise violence, and control the gateway to virtually every form of power and source of stability (economic, military, social).

Some expect and demand that the newly elected government founded on democratic principals take legal action against the Taliban high officials, and warlords such as Dostam, Raketi, Ali, Sayyaf, and Fahim in order to implement justice. To their dismay, the current administration not only has failed to bring such individuals to justice, it has even raised their position of power within the institutional framework of the government. The state has provided them with many opportunities to strengthen their political influence and economic muscle through using the democratic political process to their advantage.

The Struggle to Survive

To avoid further conflict and bloodshed, the government has followed a strategy that stems from the frail capacity of the center to secure control on the periphery. Therefore, as it finds itself incapable of subordinating warlords' military forces to that of its own, in many parts of Afghanistan, it adheres to the policy of accession and passivity. This conduct does not live up to many of democracy's central norms and values (respect for justice). It does not correspond to the core principles of the theory of state legitimacy either, which requires the state to be in command of law enforcement and adjudication.

In addition, the United State's foreign policy in Afghanistan, its relations with, and favorable treatment of warlords has subsequently influenced the domestic policy decisions of the Afghan government. The U.S. military and economic support of private armies has contributed to the weakening of the state's authority relative to that of the warlords. Consequently, it has made a carefully calculated decision to compromise and to avoid the occurrence of any major conflicts with its enemies and adversaries in order to stay in power.

President Karzai's base of power rests primarily among the educated and moderate Afghans with secular political tendencies. They constitute a small segment of the population with resources that could hardly match those of the warlords. Also, the Afghan government is at a great economic disadvantage compared to warlords whose primary source of income is comprised of revenues obtained from drug cultivation and trafficking. A brief comparative glance at the income generating capability of the two could plainly exhibit this point. The domestic revenue of the government in 2004 was two hundred million dollars. On the other hand, the heads of the private armed forces collected revenues in a multibillion-dollar illegal industry. One does not need to be a mathematician to comprehend the weakness of the state's economic position in comparison to the wealthy warlords' financial capacity. By means of drug-dollars, warlords literally purchase constituents' support during elections, while keeping their armed forces loyal and obedient to their authority (Ruben 2).

It is clearly demonstrable that the government has not yet created a military structure strong enough to counter the authority of the influential warlords and even some of the Taliban's high-ranking officials. Therefore, the security challenges that they pose to the current administration are indeed greater than the state's extent of power. Subsequently, their economic and military superiority forces the state to resort to a compromising position. In fact, President Karzai himself has pointed out that warlords represent "the greatest threat to Afghanistan's security . . . more dangerous than the remnants of the Taliban regime (Pan 2). What gives credibility to his statement is the fact that Afghanistan does not possess a military or police force capable of effectively disarming local power-brokers and eradicating drug production. A recent report by the

U.S. Government Accountability Office (GAO) has testified that the Afghan National Army and police force lacks adequate training and equipment necessary to effectively implement law and assure order. The report has also indicated that in the absence of a long-term integrated plan, especially between the German[60] and the American authorities, the future of the Afghan security forces remains uncertain. Furthermore, the number of embedded trainers within the army does not meet the need to sustain instruction at a rapidly progressive pace (GAO-05-575 June/05). Undoubtedly, shortcomings as such place the state at great disadvantage relative to private militia while trying to rebuild the law enforcement institutions.

The U.S. Foreign Policy

What is the impact of the U.S. foreign policy on the Afghan government's choices of rules, and courses of actions that it elects to follow? Let us not ignore the fact that the international community, lead by the United States, provides the current administration with significant political and economic support. However, it is equally important to note that while the U.S. has remained supportive of the Afghan government, it has also provided the warlords, (regardless of their history of human rights abuses) with considerable amount of economic and military aid on a steady basis. Ironically, the United States' support for private militant factions corresponds with the slow process of establishing a national army and police force.

The Bush administration's primary aim by overthrowing the Taliban's regime was to destroy Al-Qaeda's base of operations through strong military action. To achieve this, the United States' foreign policy in Afghanistan, centered on the war on terrorism platform, has established a strong foundation for warlords' and even the Taliban's participation in the recent parliamentary elections. Warlords have enjoyed political support by many high-ranking U.S. officials and military elite who perhaps feel indebt because of their assistance to the American military forces fighting against the Taliban and Al-Qaeda. As a result, following the overthrow of the Taliban government, the Afghan interim administration had little choice but to assign commanders of these private armies to positions of power and influence, trusting them with the safety and control of the general population.

This in turn, has contributed to their hold on many key political positions. The process of empowering the warlords is designed to serve United States' central foreign policy objective in Afghanistan - the war on terrorism. However, embracing this strategy has jeopardized some of its other goals: eradication of drugs and establishment of a stable political environment. In order to minimize the American casualties, from the inception of the U.S. military operations in Afghanistan, Washington decided to use Afghan militant factions as proxy warriors on the ground. It is easy to realize that many of the U.S. policy decision makers have maintained favorable views about these local

---

[60] Germany has played a major role in training the Afghan police force.

strongmen. For instance, Dana Rohrabacher[61] emphasized the value of "the guys who sided with the United States . . . Dostam, Atta, and Khan . . . the people who defeated the Taliban (Kolhatkar and Ingals 2)." It appears that representative Rohrabacher has not taken into serious consideration the accusations of horrific crimes committed by these "guys" throughout the past two decades of war.

Similarly, deputy secretary of defense, Paul Wolfowitz argued that the United States must adopt the strategy of working with "those warlords . . . to encourage good behavior (Kolhatkar and Ingals 2)." It is not clear exactly what he meant by saying "good behavior." If he was attempting to indicate submission to the laws of the state, and abstinence from drug trafficking and crime, the U.S. does not seem to have been successful at encouraging this sort of behavior among them at all.

Clearly, many of the U.S. foreign policy makers do not seem to be overly concerned about the kind of future that warlords' empowerment and rule could hold for the Afghan people. Bob Woodward's Bush at War presents a detailed account of how the American political elite deliberated, and launched the attack on Al-Qaeda and the Taliban with the intent to institute regime change in Afghanistan. Surprisingly, in this book it is difficult to find any indication of a meaningful discourse about the impact of warlords' further empowerment on the state-building efforts in Afghanistan. Sure enough, neither the news stories, nor the human rights reports from Afghanistan indicate that warlords have been, in the words of former Defense Secretary Donald Ramsfeld, "contributing to stability" since the fall of the Taliban (Kolhatkar and Ingals 2). On the contrary, by competing against the center's authority, and in many areas of the country, by monopolizing the right of violence, warlords such as Dostam, Atta, Ali, Khan, and Sayyaf are serving the exact opposite purpose of what the U.S. foreign policy has intended to achieve. Evidently, strategy preferences of the U.S. political elite, within the context of the war on terror, are of profound influence and consequences for the current Afghan administration's domestic policy. As a result, the state has not only chosen to show leniency toward warlords and former Taliban influential elites, it has even rewarded them with positions of power and prestige.

Conclusion

Since the fall of the Taliban, the Afghan government has endeavored to minimize military opposition to its authority. Therefore, it has made considerable political concessions to those accused of human rights violations, and even to the same forces it has sought to replace. Accordingly, many warlords, and some of the prominent members of the Taliban regime have had the opportunity to participate in September, 18 2005 *Wolosi Jirga* elections, and win many seats in the legislative body of the government. This is a function of the current administration's reconciliation and appeasement guideline. According to this policy, most of the former Taliban officials

---

[61] Dana Rohrabacher is the Chairman of the Oversight and Investigations Subcommittee of the House International Relations Committee. He Currently serves his ninth term in Congress, representing California's 46th District.

willing to cooperate with the Afghan government and the U.S. in the war on terrorism, have escaped prosecution, and even enjoyed the opportunity to strengthen their political influence and economic supremacy. The embracing of this policy in the light of the United States' perception of the military value of warlords has profoundly affected the democratic process in Afghanistan. Foreign policy decisions based on calculations for immediate and short-term military gains on part of the U.S. political elite have greatly contributed to the legitimacy of cooperating Taliban and warlords' authority. Reinforced by the relative military and economic limitations of the state, this has given those individuals, whom many view as criminals, the opportunity to take advantage of the newly democratic process and further their personal interests. The consequence of these choices is the weakening of the central government's authority in asserting legitimacy in practice and in principle.

CHAPTER SIX

Corruption and Drugs

A Deadly Combination Weakening the State

Har che begandad namakash mezanand
Waay ba roz e ke begandad namak

What is perishable is to be salted
Alas, when the salt itself is spoiled

(   )

"There is corruption in the whole system," said President Karzai alluding to the newly established democratic system in Afghanistan. During an interview with <u>Fortune Magazine</u> in August 2006, he admitted to institutional corruption. He also said that many state officials benefit from the well-developed illegal drug industry (Ellis 1). The public's perception matches President Karzai's observation. The involvement of civil servants in drug trade has created serious impediments on the path of the Afghan state and the international community's war against drugs. Drugs and corruption are two different, and yet intertwined issues that have posed great challenges to the creation of a sovereign and legitimate state in Afghanistan. The problem of a complex unlawful drug economy and the deep penetration of those who play crucial role in its cultivation and trade within the state's various institutional structures collaboratively reinforce each other. This reality threatens to transform Afghanistan from a *democratic* to a *narco-*state, and weaken the institutional organization of the government. Therefore, the public is unhappy and suspicious of a government perceived as under the control and in service of the corrupt officials/warlords. The lack of capacity on part of the state in implementing law, and in providing sufficient security and other social services has also spoiled the perception of the state as a sovereign entity in the eyes of the Afghans.

Clearly, utilizing a combination of granted political power and large sums of drug-dollars, corrupt state officials have skillfully placed themselves in a position above the law, which in turn, has severely damaged the legitimacy and sovereignty of the state. This is evident in numerous media stories from Afghanistan, in which the participation of warlords in drug trade (as prominent state employees) is the central theme. These reports mainly focus on the involvement of chiefs of police, governors, and even ministers in drug trade and other illegal activities. The accused officials have failed to serve the public giving priority to their own self-interest at the expense of the public's social, political, and economic welfare. Largely, this reality is the result of a joint policy embraced by the Afghan and the U.S. decision makers. They have chosen to reward warlords in return for their collaboration in the war on terror.[62] The strategy of appeasing warlords comes in direct clash with the state and the international community's objectives of eradicating drugs and corruption in Afghanistan.

Institutional Corruption

While a study conducted by Jakob Svensson[63] points out the difficulty of finding an exact definition for it, he has been successful in summarizing the main aspects of public corruption. Svenson defines this type of corruption simply as the "misuse of public office for private gain" (20). Numerous incidents of power abuse by the state officials are testimony to the proper application of this phenomenon in Afghanistan. This description corresponds with the behavior of warlords who have captured political power at various public institutions. A glance at some of these cases confirms the relevance of the public corruption in Afghanistan to Svenson's characterization of it: "The sale of government property by government officials, kickbacks in public procurement, bribery and embezzlement of government funds" are examples of various types of corruption that clearly apply to his definition of this term (20).

Despite the formation of a new democratic system, abuse of power by the politician-warlords broadens the meaning of corruption further to include gross human rights violations. Freedom House[64] in an on-line article about Afghans' political rights and civil liberties finds "government ministers as well as warlords" responsible for authorizing "widespread abuses by the police, military, and intelligence forces under their command" (6). Arbitrary arrests and detentions, torture, extortion, and extra judicial killings are examples of the ways in which warlords in control of law enforcement treat the civilian population. This explains the high number (2000) of complaints about human rights violations filed by AIHRC during June-December 2004 (6). The nature of these complaints perfectly matches the kinds of crimes that have reportedly been committed by the state authorities nationwide. Thus, the definition of public corruption, in the case of Afghanistan expands beyond the misuse of power for personal gain. It encompasses acts of violence that seriously threaten the lives and fundamental liberties of civilians.

See chapter three for a detailed discussion on the policy of appeasement toward warlords by the Afghan administration and the United States.

[63] Jakob Svensson is assistant professor at the Institute for International Economic Studies – Stockholm University, Sweden. He is also senior economist with Development Research Group, World Bank. Washington D.C.

[64] The organization's official website describes it as "a non-profit, nonpartisan organization, is a clear voice for democracy and freedom around the world. Through a vast array of international programs and publications, Freedom House is working to advance the remarkable worldwide expansion of political and economic freedom." To obtain further information, visit:
< http://www.freedomhouse.org/template.cfm?page=1>.

How does institutional corruption thrive and continue to remain a serious challenge to the state's authority? One of the main factors contributing to its vivid presence within the organizational framework of the state is the penetration of illegal drugs economy in the public sector. The correlation between corruption and drugs is prominent when high-ranking government officials seek to benefit from poppy cultivation and its trade to international markets. They have taken a leading role in protecting the drug industry's interests through a complex network of business and personal relationships established both at home and abroad. Warlords' operations include, but are not exclusive to, buying large quantities of drugs and subsequently shipping them abroad through the porous borders that Afghanistan shares with six other countries (Goodhand 205).

The unholy alliance between warlords and law enforcement officials is based on a calculated rational decision. In a country with ineffectual law enforcement capabilities, the rewards for trafficking drugs are high relative to the associated risks of arrest and punishment. The prospect for failure is minimal because warlords are mainly successful in dramatically reducing it through an extensive system of bribery founded on tribal, religious, ethnic and political ties.

Lack of Accountability

What makes the issue of the state officials' connection to drugs further interesting is that most reports from Afghanistan *implicate, allege, suspect,* and notice *indications* of connection between the exploitation of the public office and drug trade. Some even issue warnings that this country is on the verge of turning into a narco-state. However, seldom a report or news story spells out the names of high-level officials accused of corruption or drug trafficking. One could safely assume that fear of persecution by powerful warlords and politicians has discouraged some journalists from pursuing stories of corruption at high-level public sector, and deterred honest state officials from publicly mentioning any names relating to these crimes. The sophisticated networking capability among warlords and corrupt politicians has also proved effective in countering the investigative efforts of the state and the media. Whatever the reason may be, there is certainly no or little explicit mention of influential political personalities' names linked to corruption and drugs.

For instance, a story by the Sunday Telegraph quotes Habibullah Qaderi, the anti-drug minister that "some cabinet ministers in Afghanistan are deeply implicated in the drugs trade and could be diverting foreign aid to trafficking" (1). The report affirms that Mr. Qaderi could not deny the fact that at the cabinet level corruption is related to the lucrative business of illegal drugs. However, neither the Sunday Telegraph, nor Mr. Qaderi himself could specifically identify any cabinet members associated with drugs. Without mentioning the name of even one suspected official, another news story published by the Boston Globe also suggests that drugs are "fueling corruption at the highest levels of government" (Bernard 1). While this statement suggests a cause and effect relationship between drugs and institutional corruption, it does not specify any official's name regarding this association.

Two questions are worthy of contemplation: Firstly, what does "highest levels of government exactly mean? Secondly, is the government simply unable, or is it able but disinclined to separate warlords from officials committed only to serving the public and loyal to the state? The answer relates to both, political will and certain capabilities required for success in the war against drugs and corruption. The challenges of mere survival and struggle to maintain peace have played key role in shaping the state's strategy of appeasement, and principally, unconditional reconciliation with warlords. Perhaps, for this reason, the Interior Ministry is reluctant to release a list of officials' names allegedly involved in the drug industry.[65]

Law Enforcement

Corruption at the lower official levels and among law enforcement officers seems to have been better recognized by media and exposed to the public.[66] Most likely, direct interaction between the public and the police amounts to greater exposure of crime and abuse of power at local level, which leads to subsequent accessibility by the media. Close encounter between the two has lead to the realization that many law enforcement agents misuse their granted powers violating the rights and liberties of the society in order to protect their own self-interests.

Reflecting this perception is the opinion of an entrepreneur from Kabul who thinks, "more than 90 percent of the police are corrupt" (Ibrahimi 1). His experience with the law enforcement agents may have influenced the way his view of the state institutions is shaped. Immediately, after the robbery of his store, he had found a police officer's identity card on the premises. As he reported this incident to the authorities, the police threatened him that his life would be in danger if he told this story to any one else (Ibrahimi 1). It is difficult to blame this man for perceiving the police force as untrustworthy since apparently it had failed to ensure the obedience of its own officers to the rule of law.

Such incident of looting by the police is not an isolated event or an exception to the rule. Police breaks the law in variety of other ways, including active involvement in drug trafficking. It is no secret that cooperation between the police (many of whom are former warlords) and other warlords has impeded the government and international community's efforts in the fight against drugs and terror. Media has uncovered stories of the involvement of the government's mid-tier law enforcement agents in drug trade numerous times.

---

65 Moreau, Ron. and Sami Yousafzai. "A Harvest of Treachery: Afghanistan's drug trade is threatening the stability of a nation America went to war to stabilize. What can be done?" Newsweek May 2005 <http://www.msnbc.msn.com/id/10663339/>.

66 CNN, New York Times, Daily Telegraph, Toronto Sun, Washington Post, Pajwok Afghan News and Kabul Press are a few examples of various forms of news media that have widely reported on the issue of police and military involvement in drug trade.

For instance, on July 24, 2006 Pajhwok, an Afghan news agency, reported the arrest of the intelligence chief of Rostaq district in Takhar province for drug position and trafficking.[67] He was captured with 5Kg of heroin and two Kalashnikovs that he had allegedly planned to smuggle to Tajikistan in a government vehicle. This arrest is a shining, or perhaps not so shining, example of institutional corruption, which gives reason to many Afghans not to count on the integrity of the state.

Other reports also indicate that the police illegally levy taxes on the traffickers of drugs and growers of opium. Among many, Global and Mail has published testimonies by the smugglers and farmers of opium to illustrate unlawful conduct by the police. Two opium traffickers admitted that they regularly bribed the police in order to maintain their operations uninterrupted (Greame 1). They persistently dedicated 4 to 20 percent of their income to these payments in return for permission to breach the law without having to face any consequences. According to the same article, bribing the police is common among the growers of poppy as well. The police usually forces farmers to pay "a flat rate that is the equivalent of $5800 to $7000 a year" depending on the size of the field, networking ability of the farmers with corrupt officials, and the market value of poppy (Greame 1). This allows the farmers to successfully harvest their crops of poppy and safely supply it to the warlords. Clearly, these cases depict an association between drugs and institutional corruption. The relationship between the two creates a bond that further strengthens the power of warlords at the expense of weakening the authority of the state. This weakening occurs in tangible terms – undermining state power to tax, implement regulations, and manage the economy. It also entails political ramifications. In turn, the public views the state's authority as being compromised. In addition, within the large poppy cultivation areas, the state looses claim to the management and distribution of resources, which results in damaging the legitimacy of the state.[68]

Corruption has exacerbated the already difficult predicament that the state faces while proceeding with its campaign against drugs. The Executive Director of the United Nations Office on Drugs and Crime (UNODC), Antonio Maria Costa argues that in Afghanistan the issue of the war on drugs could remain more challenging than ever because of problems such as "renewed insecurity [and] continued corruption" (U.N. News Service 1). Having understood what corruption in the context of this country's current political and economic conditions means, Mr. Costa's argument seems highly plausible mainly because all three issues of drugs, corruption and insecurity seem to have remained intertwined. It is evident that the revenues generated through drug cultivation and trade support dishonest state officials. Subsequently, the officials not only refrain from taking action against the warlords, but also protect their interests. The potential for enormous economic gains through involvement in drug trade serves as a great incentive for warlords and corrupt state officials, equipped with weapons, work force and connections to risk low probability of arrest and punishment.

---

[67] Sarfaraz, Abdul Mateen. Pajhwok Afghan News July 24, 2006
< http://www.pajhwak.com/viewstory.asp?lng=eng&id=21662>.
[68] See chapter seven: "Impact of Drug Trade on State Legitimacy."

While drug economy damages the reputation of the state in the eyes of the public, it funds not only warlords, but also Al-Qaeda and Taliban's political campaign and military operations against the government.[69] This has ultimately resulted in great harm to state's authority throughout the country. Robert B. Charles, Assistant Secretary of State for International Drug and Law Enforcement has confirmed that the proceeds from drug trade primarily benefit the three major enemies of the state mentioned above (Carpenter 4). The realities of this situation suggest that there is a strong contradiction between state's policy of compromising with the warlords and its efforts to combat drugs and corruption.

A joint report by the Pentagon and the State Department names one of the main types of corruption common within the police force as "bribe and release."[70] This simply means that those under arrest and detention bribe the police officers, buying their way out of the grip of the law. The report emphasizes that this custom undermines the authority of the state. According to The Baltimore Sun, it therefore intensifies "pervasive corruption" among police force as one of the main "obstacles facing the $1.1 billion training program at work to establish an effective law enforcement agency in Afghanistan (1). It indeed is difficult to rule out the $3 billion drug industry as one of the potential sources contributing to funds utilized to bribe the police. In fact, the insidious nature of corruption is a strong indication of a correlation between it and drugs' trafficking in Afghanistan.

Taking advantage of their political influence, many of the state's leading authorities have decided to benefit from the drug industry through collaboration with, rather than resistance against its operators. This has had a highly counter-productive impact on the anti-drug measures taken by the Afghan government and the international community. The UNODC draws this conclusion emphasizing that "corruption principally at the level of provincial governors, has been one of the major impediments to counter-drug activities" (Sedra 9). Among others, counter drug efforts include compiling intelligence reports, as well as investigation, arrest and prosecution of drug-lords in each province. However, unwillingness on the part of a governor to cooperate in taking an active role in costly and difficult anti-drug operations is certainly diminishing the likelihood of the operations' success. The 2006 Afghanistan Opium Survey has estimated that only 57% of the governors' claims of eradication are verifiable. The report noticeably indicates that largely the efforts to combat drugs have failed.[71]

Recently, the new Chief Justice, Abdul Jabbar Sabet accused the governor of Herat province of corruption and exploitation of public office. During a conference in London, he said that in Herat, there has been an increase in "looting of public wealth"

[69] Mili. Hayder, and Jacob Townsed. "Global Terrorism Analysis: Afghanistan's Drug Trade and How it Funds Taliban Operations." The Jamestown Foundation May 10, 2007. Vol. 5, Issue 9.

[70] See "U.S. Report Faults Readiness of Afghanistan's Police Force." The Baltimore Sun Dec 5 2006: <http://www.baltimoresun.com/news/>.

[71] See Afghanistan Opium Survey 2006 Executive Summary prepared by the UNODC and the Afghan Ministry of Counter Drug. Sep 2006.

while the governor has been busy conducting his own business exploiting the public office. Sabet indicted the governor and his officers with public corruption and millions of dollars in tax evasion. He has also assured the public that justice will be served in the case of the mayor of Herat city Muhammad Rafiq Mujaddidi, a relative of Sebghatullah Mujaddidi, the head of the National Reconciliation Commission (NRC).

Rafiq Mujaddidi is accused of misuse of the public office and collaboration with the governor of Herat in unspecified illicit activities. Sabet claims that he is currently making efforts to bring both men to justice, but is facing swift opposition from Sebghatullah Mujaddidi (Popal 2). This serves as a vivid example of efforts by a state official in creating hindrances in the path of institutional reform and transparency. Therefore, more measures that are serious seem necessary in order to address the issue of institutional corruption. These measures would inevitably mean transformation of state's policy in regards to warlords and their official collaborators. In so far, relative to the scope of public corruption and the impact of drug trade on the Afghan political economy, the efforts leading to permanently resolving these matters seem sporadic and ineffectual in magnitude as well as in substance.

According to the testimonies by victims and witnesses of various crimes, corruption within the police force and military has also entailed gross human rights abuses. Implicating corruption and crime, a 101 page report prepared by Human Rights Watch contains numerous accounts of disregard for the rule of law by the agents of the state. It is no wonder that this report is appropriately titled "Killing You is a Very Easy Thing for Us: Human Rights Abuses in Southeast Afghanistan."[72]

Based on this study as well as news reports from Afghanistan, police officers at various levels not only have failed to fulfill their duty by preventing traffickers from smuggling heroin across the country's borders, but also actively participated in its production and trade. Their participation in this industry has taken place in two principal forms. They have either allowed the production, processing and transportation of drugs in return for bribe, or personally participated in these illegal acts.

An investigative report by the Christian Science Monitor clearly demonstrates the involvement of police in drug trade. This report is the outcome of a series of interviews initially taped without the interviewee's knowledge and permission in order to encourage the subjects to "speak more casually and loosely than they would, if they knew they were speaking to a reporter" (Baldauf 4). The interviews took place in Takhar province (the final destination for drug traders before crossing the border over to Tajikistan) during which police officers of various ranks revealed to the reporters details of their direct and indirect involvement in the industry.

Among police chiefs, commander Dost proudly admitted of becoming "a dangerous smuggler" (2). He supported his argument by admitting that he had smuggled hundreds of thousands of dollars worth of heroin to Tajikistan. How a police chief could be successful at risky operations as such? According to Dost, the key element in answering this question is *connection*. He has established business relationships with

---

[72] To view the complete report on-line, visit:
<http://www.hrw.org/reports/2003/afghanistan0703/>.

other police, military, as well as civil service officials leading to the formation of a strong drug trade network. This network has helped him evade danger and continue to commit crime. Dost has been caught with as much as $370,000 worth heroin, and yet released shortly after utilizing a combination of money and personal ties with other police officers to buy his freedom. Interestingly, Dost has stated that his case is not an aberration: "These prosecutors do it themselves. [They smuggle] 300 to 400 kilos each time," he said complaining that higher-ranking state officials have proven to be astute business competitors (Baldauf 1). This is clearly an indication of the severity of drugs' corrupting impact across law enforcement institutions.

Monitor's reporters interviewed Commander Nasir as well. His business association with other Afghan police chiefs has required maintaining personal relationships with the help of large amounts of cash. Adding different sums of bribes that he had given to a Northern Alliance commander throughout the years, Nasir said that he had paid him alone $680,000 to ensure the success of his operations (Baldauf 2). Commander Dost and Nasir's stories are only two of the numerous other cases in which large sums of money change hands among commanders, corrupt government officials and traffickers to make the illegal trade of drugs possible.

The high cost associated with drug trade is an indication of high-income generating opportunity available to the police and warlords. Some of the top police officers are not content with as much as "$20,000 a night from drug money," said Ahmad Noor, another corrupt police commander from Takhar (Baldauf 3). The monetary rewards for illegal drug trade seem extremely high in a relatively manageable and low risk environment.

Police involvement in drug trade is not limited to high-level officials. Many soldiers are also used to taking petty bribes from drug traffickers on regular basis. "I will get $10,000 from him, but that poor soldier standing there will accept $200 from the smuggler," said commander Bilal to Monitor's interviewers (Baldauf 4). Evidence as such point to a strong correlation between corruption and drugs, one reinforcing the other.

While corruption and drug's dual operations entail the involvement of low and mid-level government employees, the participation of the state's officials in such activities could reach as high as the Ministry of Interior, Afghanistan's supreme law enforcement agency. This mainly takes place in one of the two major forms. The first entails taking of large amounts of bribe money by the bureaucratic elite in exchange for lucrative employment opportunities in the ministry – in Kabul and other provinces.[73] "Almost all of the police commanders in Takhar have paid officials at the Interior Ministry to get their jobs," said commander Bilal (Baldauf 4). This indicates the breadth of corruption and its relationship to drug trade within one of the major law enforcement agencies.

What determines the value of these opportunities in terms of potential monetary gains is a desirable location? The areas in and around the higher concentration of poppy

---

[73] Author's interview with some of the state employees whom have been deployed to the U.S. to receive training and education.

fields are obviously desirable for higher probability of generating more income through illegal taxation, extortion and bribery. Furthermore, territories in the proximity of the country's borders with any one of its Central and South Asian neighbors are of higher potential income value for corrupt police officers. Hence, one of the ways in which upper level officials could benefit from drug economy is through selling positions of illegal income prospective to whoever is willing to pay the price. This is an important factor, deteriorating the state's authority, because it directly links institutional corruption to illegal trade and production of drugs.

The second way in which ministry officials take part in drug industry is by direct participation in its smuggling process. Some argue that the level at which corruption corresponds to this industry is extremely high, involving "80% of the personnel at the Ministry of Interior" (Baldauf 4). As strong indications of the severity of corruption's contaminating spread throughout the state's apparatus, statistics as such demonstrate the Afghan democratic system's poor health. Public research has not been conducted in regards to this issue. However, widespread public corruption, especially within the law enforcement agencies of the state, has not proven helpful in creating a bridge founded on the principles of trust and honesty between the people and the state.

Corruption has lead to dissatisfaction not only among the public, but among some of the faithful public officials as well. One relevant example in this regard is the show of discontent by the former Minister of Interior, Ali Ahmad Jalali. Jalali resigned from his post claiming that "unspecified government officials were involved in the opium industry" (Smith 2). He based this accusation on intelligence reports and a list of 100 key officials suspected of drug trafficking (Baldauf 4). Understanding the political sensitivity of the issue, Jalali has casually said, "sometimes [government officials] give protection to traffickers" (Harden 1). In the light of realities concerning institutional corruption, his carefully structured statement certainly understates the challenges that the Afghan government faces in resolving this problem. As customary in cases of corruption linked to drug trade, the names of these officials remain secret. One could easily view this as another blow to state's struggle claiming transparency and commitment to accountability. Lack of a genuine effort among many of its officials and institutions in creating a translucent political environment has lead to the erosion of people's confidence in the willingness and competence of state in serving the public.

While Jalali argues that Afghanistan lacks the "investigative capacity" to fight corruption effectively, Habibullah Qaderi, the Minister for Counter Narcotics insists on taking immediate action in removing the perpetrators individually from the current political system. Qaderi believes that the sooner the deletion of corrupt officials takes place, the less danger they are able to pose to the entire organization and legitimacy of the state. There are differences between Jalali and Qaderi's assessment of the strategizing capability of the government in response to this issue. However, both Jalali, and Qaderi agree that corruption ultimately separates the people from the state impairing the institutional capacity of the government in its attempt to eradicate drugs.

The main outcome of corruption, in fact, seems to be just that – alienation of the public from the state. People's awareness in regards to these matters partially stems from a relatively free press environment, and largely, the pervasiveness of crimes committed at various institutional levels. The public witnesses the involvement of civil servants and law enforcement agents in drug trade on daily basis.[74] Afghans observe bribery, and experience discriminatory treatment based on ethnic, tribal and sectarian ties. They also witness disregard for the rule of law by the agents of the state who are supposed to obey and enforce it themselves. Therefore, not only the impact of inefficiency in governance but also a high degree of unaccountability on part of the state constitutes the basis for public disenchantment.

People have expressed anger and discontent reacting to the conduct of the state officials and employees in many provinces. For example, on March 7, 2005 residents of Mazar-e-Sharif participated in demonstrations demanding the resignation of Ata Muhammad Nur, the governor of Balkh province. They claimed that Nur had illegally confiscated private land for his own personal use (Tarzi 1). They also insisted that the government appointed Nur to help ensure security of life and property for the public - not to threaten it. In spite of such demonstrations, these issues have not been investigated, and Mr. Nur continues to remain in power as governor of Balkh.

A point noteworthy is that although people have charged Nur with misuse of the public office, they view *the state* ultimately responsible for his unlawful conduct, and expect *it* to hold him accountable. As the state fails to meet people's expectations, its authority continues to remain compromised. Thus, Nur's case serves as a perfect example of a corrupt official damaging the influence of the state not only by breaking the laws he is appointed to help enforce, but also through escaping accountability for any wrongdoing altogether.

Illegal conduct in different institutions shows that public corruption is not exclusively limited to a few incidents by a handful of corrupt officials. Corruption, reinforced by drug money is pervasive in virtually all state institutions. President Karzai himself has admitted publicly that corruption is widespread in the public sector, and expressed great interest in uprooting it from all state apparatus:

> If we don't get rid of corruption in Afghanistan, the progress and development that we hope to achieve -- the prosperity that we wish for our people -- will not be achieved in Afghanistan. So, in order to improve our lives from the conditions that we have today, it is necessary for our administration to become healthier. This means that corruption must be removed from all national, provincial, and local administrations. Honesty and transparency must be established.[75]

Karzai's statement illustrates the depth of his understanding of the socio-economic ramifications of corruption in the public sector. However, until now it has

---

[74] Based on author's interview with many Afghans recently arriving to the U.S. from Afghanistan.

[75] Afghan President Hamed Karzai met with the director of <u>Radio Free Afghanistan</u> Akbar Ayazi, for a wide-ranging interview in Kabul on November 9 2006.

been clear that the state's response or lack of it to institutional corruption and drug trade has been contradictory to the goals it claims to struggle for, and therefore largely ineffective.

Conclusion

The interplay of drugs and corruption forms a deadly combination restraining state's efforts to assert authority in Afghanistan. The collaborative operation between the two is paradoxical to the moral principles of the Afghan society. Duplicity by the state officials translates into dishonesty on part of the state itself. Corrupt police officers, judges and lawmakers do little or nothing to prevent the farming of poppy and or trafficking of drugs. In fact, many facilitate its operations by joining hands with warlords. This is mainly because the economic incentives in exchange for cooperation with drug lords are extremely high. A police officer, whose salary ranges from $40 to $60 a month, could earn well over $10,000 during the same period through cooperating with traffickers and warlords. Dishonest officials realize that the prospect for their arrest, prosecution, and punishment is miniscule relative to the potential for economic rewards they hope to gain. Mr. Jalali shares this view stating that, "in Afghanistan, corruption is a low risk enterprise" (Harnden 1). Indeed, the risk of involvement in drugs industry is low mainly because the state has not taken any serious measure against those who break the law.

Allowing warlords to rule has proven contradictory to state's efforts in eliminating the illegal drug economy. They have refused to disarm their militia and are active participants in drugs smuggling. As demonstrated in this chapter, President Karzai himself, the former Interior Minister Sayed Akbar Jalali, and some of the U.N. and U.S. high-ranking officials have acknowledged that this is a real problem threatening the security of Afghanistan and the very existence of the state. It renders the state incapable of effective governance in practice as well as principle. Serving the public and protecting its interests effectively is an essential element in legitimizing the state's power. The other imperative element in this respect is the plausibility of its moral justification to govern. The commitment of crimes by state officials involving drugs and corruption exerts a damaging effect on the capacity of state to serve the public, and pronounce its rule legitimate on ethical grounds.

Corruption has certainly not helped strengthen state's control of its own institutions. This reality is reflective of its incapacity to efficiently deliver social services, and ensure the security of the people. Therefore, the ineffectiveness of its efforts to defend the public against the drug-lords' and police aggression has raised serious questions concerning its moral authority and the legitimacy of its rule among the Afghans.

CHAPTER SEVEN

Impact of Drug Trade on State Legitimacy

How serious is the threat of drug trade to the political stability of Afghanistan? Illegal cultivation and trade of drugs, combined with perpetuating institutional corruption, has profoundly affected the state in various manners. While drug economy damages the reputation of the state in the eyes of the public, it funds not only warlords, but also Al-Qaeda and Taliban's political campaign and military operations against the government.[76] This has ultimately resulted in great harm to state authority throughout the country. Robert B. Charles, Assistant Secretary of State for International Drug and Law Enforcement has confirmed that the proceeds from drug trade primarily benefit the three major enemies of the state mentioned above (Carpenter 4). The realities of this situation suggest that there is a strong contradiction between state's policy of compromising with warlords and its efforts to combat drugs and corruption.

Organizations such as the Drug Policy Alliance contend that drug trade funds the Taliban and Al Qaeda's terrorist and anti-government operations.[77] They believe that there exists a connection between the intensification of the insurgency's military operations and the rise in poppy cultivation and trade. John Boit, who has worked on a Defense Department counter-drug training project in Afghanistan, agrees that together illegal drugs and terrorism impede the U.S. Afghan efforts to combat terrorism.[78] In an article published by the Baltimore Sun, he argues that drug revenues "are used to finance terrorism that is killing our troops overseas and that could ultimately be used to fund acts of violence in the United States" (1). This line of reasoning emphasizes the seriousness of the dangers that drug trade poses to security situation in Afghanistan as well as abroad.

Furthermore, the key operators of drug economy, as participants in the current political process, undermine state's authority in collecting taxes from other legal sectors. Largely unchallenged, traders of drugs have established an illicit economy within a legal system of free enterprise and trade. The state has suffered as this illegal industry has inhibited the government's control of, and the ability to manage the economy as a whole. Consequently, drug trade has rendered state's efforts ineffective to

---

[76] Mili. Hayder, and Jacob Townsed. "Global Terrorism Analysis: Afghanistan's Drug Trade and How it Funds Taliban Operations." The Jamestown Foundation May 10, 2007. Vol. 5, Issue 9.

[77] See "Experts Tackle U.S. Drug Policy in Afghanistan." May 1, 2007.
< http://www.drugpolicy.org/news/050107afghan.cfm>.

[78] See "Evidence for the Link Between Drugs and Terrorism." July 19, 2004
<http://www.drugpolicy.org/global/terrorism/>.

implement economic development policies and to provide the population with sufficient and quality services.[79] What Afghans expect is for the state to address issues such as provision of healthcare, education, clean water, electricity and roads in an effectual and speedy manner.[80] Among others, addressing the question of drugs cultivation and trafficking could prove effective in helping the government to meet these expectations. This in turn, could lead to gaining their trust and respect – two of the necessary elements for recognition of the state as a legitimate body.

The weakness of the state represents another aspect of drugs' political impact. Revenues generated through drug trade have enabled the newly empowered politician-warlords to undermine the credibility of the state. The negative political implications of this industry are the result of the way in which it operates and sustains itself.

Primarily, drug economy benefits the rich and exploits the poor, leading to further widening of an already existing gap between the two. This rift, separating the politician-warlords from the rest of the population, has created a sub-system of economic dependency founded on a client-patron relationship between the traffickers, landowners and politician-warlords on one hand, and the poor landless peasants on the other. As a result, to ensure survival, the majority of the rural poor population has become dependent on, and to a great extent, collaborated with the minority rich in command. The poor has been forced to accept warlords' authority, rather than that of the state's, as the supreme power in charge of resource distribution. Therefore, it seems reasonable to conclude that drug economy has not only weakened, but also, significantly transferred state authority to the warlords.

This transfer of authority is specifically dependent on the ability of warlords to penetrate within the institutional organization of the state, while simultaneously managing the day-to-day operations of their illegal commercial undertakings. Politician-warlords utilize their formal and informal basis of power to avoid trouble with the law, and to increase the already high monetary gains obtained through various illegitimate ventures.

It is therefore not surprising to note that the revenues generated through drug trafficking hardly contribute to the social and economic well-being of the ordinary Afghans. In fact, drug revenues have the exact opposite effect on the economy, pulling the country "into a bottomless pit of destruction and despair."[81] This is evident in the latest statistical data published jointly by the United Nations Office on Drugs and Crime, and the Afghan Ministry of Counter Narcotics warning that the Afghan economy is following a path that leads only to additional political and social destabilization:

---

[79] Rohde, David. and David E. Sanger, "How a 'Good War' in Afghanistan Went Bad." New York Times Aug. 12, 2007. <http://www.nytimes.com>.

[80] Grazelkowski. Brian, and George Devendorf. "Bridging the Expectations Gap in Afghanistan." Mercy Corps August 7, 2007 <http://www.mercycorps.org/?sections_url=countries&subsections_url=afghanistan&items_id=1787&>.

[81] See the preface to "Afghanistan Opium Survey 2006" by Antonio Maria Costa, the Executive Director of UNODC.

> This year [2006] opium cultivation rose to 165000
> hectares, a 59% increase over 2005. An unprecedented
> 6100 tons of opium has been harvested, making
> Afghanistan virtually the sole supplier to the world (1).

Drug' illegal trade, intertwined with public corruption, takes place at such phenomenal scale that it has certainly transformed the Afghan economy into a narco-economic system. As the world's largest producer of opium the country's global production rate alarmingly increased to 92% in 2006.[82] This certainly is a serious threat to the political, economic and social stability of the country, and subsequently the legitimacy of the Afghan state.

Disparity

One of the internal ramifications of the drug economy is its impact on the increase in disparity between the rich warlords, and the majority poor population. Deep economic rift between the two entails a significant political consequence that affects all aspects of the Afghans' life – social, political and economic. It has perpetuated dependency of the poor on powerful warlords and rich traffickers. Subsequently, this dependency has alienated and discouraged the poor from reliance on and cooperation with the state. Many have to turn to warlords for protection and access to resources. Formation of this patron-client relationship is fundamentally based on the ability of warlords to compete against the state over the right to monopolize violence as well as the ability to control and distribute scarce resources.

It is important to remember that this arrangement exists within a society struck by decades of continuous war and abject poverty. It has been well established that in spite of international community's investment in, and dedication of enormous efforts to reconstruction of Afghanistan, it continues to remain one of the bottom ten poorest countries in the world. According to a report released in February 2005 by the United Nations Development Program (UNDP), Afghanistan ranks 175th among 177 nations on the Human Poverty Index (HPI).[83] This report thoroughly discusses the Afghans' poor quality of life based on human security, social injustice and economic disparity, scarcity of opportunity, the lack of basic human needs and the critically dysfunctional state of the educational system. It clearly demonstrates that Afghanistan is one of the least developed countries on the international arena.

As it becomes evident that only 28.7 percent of the population is literate, the privation level at which society struggles looses its element of surprise.[84] The UNDP

---

[82] See <u>Afghanistan Opium Survey 2006 Executive Summary</u>: "Summary of Findings." This survey is the result of joint efforts by the United Nations Office on Drugs and Crime and Afghan Ministry of Counter Drug. Sep. 2006.
[83] See Tajbakhsh et al Pg. 11
[84] See Tajbakhsh et al Pg.12

report paints a vivid picture of the severity of the socio-economic conditions in Afghanistan by comparing the life expectancy of the Afghans (44.5 years at birth) with that of its neighboring populations as well as other *least* developed countries of the world. Life expectancy in Afghanistan, where 50 percent of its people lives in poverty, is "at least 20 years lower than all of its neighboring countries, [and] remains 6.1 years lower than the average of the least developed countries."[85] In a society where "one out of five children dies before the age of five, and one woman dies from pregnancy related causes every thirty minutes," life expectancy at such low level could only be expected.[86]

In addition, after a thorough study of this report, it is easy to understand the conditions in which many Afghan women struggle (mostly unsuccessfully) to survive, suffering from maternal mortality rates "60 times higher than for women in industrial countries."[87] The facts presented above clearly exhibit that the Afghans are an extremely poor nation. Unfortunately, as in many underdeveloped countries, in Afghanistan too the plight of poverty exerts its greatest impact on women and children.

While many struggle with financial destitute, ironically, statistics show that conditions at macro-economic level have tremendously improved and continued to do so. A study conducted by the British Department of International Development demonstrates that the Afghan economy reached a 29% growth level in 2002. Since then, it has continued to grow each year. Many observers are convinced that the economy will carry on this upward trend for many years to follow. In fact, the same report makes mention of the Afghan government's forecast, according to which, on average within the next decade Afghanistan will achieve an overall 9% economic growth. Based on the study's prediction, this pattern of success seems sufficient to increase the average annual per capita income from $300 to $500 (2). While the statistical data presented above appear impressive, it is important not to forget that economic growth does not necessarily guarantee economic justice, and or a higher standard of living for all. In other words, overall growth at macroeconomic level does not necessarily translate into poverty mitigation. Until now, according to Afghanistan Independent Human Rights Commission report, released in May 2006, the overall macro-economic growth has done little to alleviate poverty and shorten the distance between the rich and the poor.[88]

In spite of the billions of dollars spent by the international community to reconstruct Afghanistan, a vast majority of people continue to live in abject poverty. Analysts find various factors responsible for the persistence of destitution in Afghanistan. Some believe that lack of, or inefficiency in communication, coordination and cooperation among NGOs, as well as between international organizations and the Afghan government has lead to inadequate results. Others primarily find faulty policy formulations on the part of both, the governmental and non-governmental organizations guilty of rendering the aid projects less effective than initially hoped, and expected. It is

---

[85] See Tajbakhsh et al Pg.12

[86] See Tajbakhsh et al Pg. 13

[87] See Tajbakhsh et al Pg. 13

[88] See "Economic and Social Rights in Afghanistan: Summary Report." Afghanistan Independent Human Rights Commission May 2006.

also clear that institutional corruption in various forms, such as favoritism, nepotism, bribery, embezzlement of funds, and irresponsible expenditure, has seriously damaged the efforts to reconstruct Afghanistan and help the needy.

Additionally, some see the shortage of skilled and experienced Afghans primarily responsible for the slow pace of progress in improving the plight of the poor. Many recognize this phenomenon, often applied to the socio-economic realities of developing countries, as the brain-drain theory.[89] Perhaps, taking the combined effects of all these factors into account, a thorough study could explain the persistence of poverty among this war-ravaged nation.

Nevertheless, it is equally important to note that extreme destitute exists among a large number of the Afghan population within a unique context. The new political and economic arrangements have given rise to new power structures as well as new resource distribution systems, within which the right to control and manage wealth is almost exclusively allocated to politician-warlords. This has countered the objectives desired by the separation of powers, and the creation of a scheme based on the democratic institutional fundamentals (checks and balances), allowing warlords to ensure domination on both, political and economic grounds. The foundation of this power distributing framework mainly lies on the cultivation and trafficking of opium. Subsequently, at an avoidable cost of day-to-day suffering by the millions of ordinary Afghans, a handful of warlords and corrupt government officials benefit from this arrangement.

Yet, it is important to note that the impact of drug economy is not simply limited to the economic hardship among the majority. The increase in warlords' might, as primary traders of drugs, rigorously affects the Afghan political economy in two other manners. First, warlords' power rooted in drug production and trade has undermined the political legitimacy of the state. Secondly, a combination of factors, such as the alleged commitment of current and past crimes and corrupt practices by taking advantage of public office amount to the projection of the state's image as a feeble, corrupt and ineffectual organ. These conditions, unfavorable to the welfare of the society and the authority of the state, have forced the civilian population to remain aloof from the state and become dependent on warlords in order to survive.

---

[89] In an article titled "A Brain Drain Threatens Afghanistan's Future," Obaid Younossi discusses how the Afghan government could not only prevent the flight of educated, skilled and talented Afghans from the Afghanistan, but also invite more of them to return and serve their country. Younossi is a senior analyst at the Rand Corporation, a nonprofit research organization. To read this article, visit: <www.rand.org/commnetary/020906IHT.html>.

Inequality

The gap between the rich and the poor is highly visible in every one of the major cities of Afghanistan – Kabul, Kandahar, Herat and Mazar e Sharif, as well as in most rural parts of the country. Whether involved in poppy cultivation or not, millions of Afghans continue to struggle to survive living in the inner city slums, or mud-huts in the villages. They remain deprived of the basic life amenities such as clean water, food and shelter. They also lack the kind of political knowledge, organization, and networking capabilities empowering them to counterbalance the monopoly of warlords on social, political and economic resources. In contrast, warlords and corrupt state officials reside in some of the most elegantly designed multi-story mansions surrounded by painfully manicured gardens.[90]

Witnesses to such disparity in living conditions between the slums and the mansions, which is an accurate reflection of the existing economic inequality, describe such scenes as unbelievably appalling. The Daily Telegraph in an article titled "Afghanistan Crisis Paves Way for Return of the Taliban," views the manifestation of such deep inequality within the Afghan society as an "affront to the eyes" (3). These socio-economic imbalances seem to be primarily responsible for consequences that have traditionally followed scarcity of resources and social injustice in underdeveloped countries. Distrust of and disgruntlement with the ruling elite could possibly lead to the eventual political turmoil; namely a military coup, or even a civil war.

Unsurprisingly, social scientists barely view a democratic state with a middle class minority, a handful of extremely powerful warlords, and a large number of people living in absolute poverty as an example of a healthy and stable society. Clearly, the new political organization has not yet made a significant difference in the lives of the majority of the populace. Indeed, it has been largely unsuccessful in regulating the market, let alone forming it.[91] This has lead to disappointment among the majority poor.

Furthermore, what has contributed to public restlessness is the ever-increasing power and wealth of the already rich and powerful warlords and corrupt politicians, whom often refuse to abide by the laws of the state (Miller 10). As discussed previously, a critical element in recognizing the credibility of the state is the degree to which it is capable and or willing to conform to the guidelines and abide by the same principles that it expects its subjects to follow. If the state's agents fail to respect the laws that are of its own creation, its efforts to implement those laws among the populous would most likely prove fruitless.

The establishment of a functional system and the application of effective mechanisms to manage and distribute economic resources is one of the main conditions attesting to the authority of the state. However, the economics of drug trade, and the pragmatic solutions to the question of warlords' participation in the Afghan democratic process has proven detrimental to the state's efforts in asserting legitimacy. Jonathan

---

[90] Interview with Afghans residing in Afghanistan, and those who live abroad, however, have visited the country within the past three years.

[91] See Ghani et al's list of state rights and responsibilities – chapter three.

Goodhand, senior professor of the Department of Development Studies at the University of London, categorizes one of the illegal segments of the Afghan economy as "combat economy" (203). The existence of this segment reflects on the weakness, and in many cases, absence of the state in a measurable portion of the financial sector. He argues that "production, mobilization and allocation of resources" by warlords play a key role in the creation and survival of a combat economy, which primarily depends on their ability to establish monopoly over the means of violence (203). Warlords reserve the right to make decisions as to when, why, and against whom to engage in violence. The flow of revenue from drug trade has granted them the strength to make such decisions. As a result, they guarantee security (a valuable and scarce resource) or the lack of it to the struggling local population. This serves as great impetus for attracting cooperation from the vast numbers of poverty-stricken farming communities. Economic domination and manipulation of the political system by warlords has proven detrimental to the legitimacy of the state; because it clearly demonstrates that, the state has fallen short of fulfilling some of its key responsibilities - administrative control and rule of law.

According to the theory of statehood, agreed upon by scholars such as Max Weber and John Lock, monopoly on the legitimate use of violence arms the state with the power to protect its citizens, and the capacity to formulate and implement policy. This capability helps the state to gain and maintain legitimacy. While, in theory, the power to curb or employ violence is a privilege only enjoyed by the sovereign state, in Afghanistan's political reality this authority largely lies in the hands of warlords and corrupt politicians. Although Goodhand does not ignore the role of external factors (foreign interference) in the culmination of the ideal conditions unfavorable to the state's credibility, he emphasizes the importance of drug economy as an essential element for sustaining conditions favorable to warlords (200). Utilizing a compound of power and prestige, warlords who wield enormous political influence and military might have been able to weaken, marginalize and even eliminate the state's authority in various regions of the country.[92]

Dependency

A vast majority of the poor population has little choice but to depend on warlords for the security of their lives and maintaining a minimum level of subsistence. The facts on the ground clearly demonstrate this veracity. For example, the United Nations' Afghanistan Opium Survey 2006 confirms the involvement of 44,800 households in opium cultivation during that year. The total number of three million people implicated in this industry has never been as high as this in the entire known history of Afghanistan (1). Therefore, one could easily deduce that the quandary of drug trade is more serious than ever before affecting social, economic and political lives of the Afghans.

---

[92] For example, Dostam continues to wield power in the north, and Hazrat Ali in eastern Nangarhar, and Noristan.

The fact that warlords serve as a link between the global markets and domestic producers has also placed them at a superior position relative to that of the landless peasants. Their rank at the top of the hierarchy of the drug economy considerably increases their share of illegal income. Warlords use these revenues to maintain their command over the means of violence, and control of resource distribution systems at regional and even national levels. This has further ensured and strengthened their grip on power, and dominance over the ordinary Afghan population, as well as the state. They rely on a "culture of impunity" to break the law in almost every imaginable form with little or no fear of prosecution by the state.[93]

Drug economy forces many farming families to accept, however low, any amount of payment in return for their poppy harvest. Furthermore, most farmers who do not own land find themselves having little choice but to rent these poppy fields from the owners and warlords at unrealistically high rates. On average, they pay 65 to 85 percent of their crops to the landowners in order to fulfill their financial obligations. This amounts to a great debt among most of the farming population in Afghanistan. While the average annual per capita income is around $200, "the average amount of debt per family is $1,150."[94] This is mainly because the landowner determines the amount of the rent based on the estimated future yield of opium, which is often impossible to materialize. Henceforth, if the revenue from the harvest falls short of meeting the projected income, the proprietor will reschedule the payment for the next season.

Scarcely any other crop has the same earning potential as opium. Therefore, in order to make payments on the accumulated debt from the past, the farmer is obligated to continue cultivating poppy the following season. This arrangement places him/her in a socio-economic deadlock. It is also noteworthy that 75 percent of the population resides in rural Afghanistan's farming communities.[95] Many continue to remain under direct or indirect influence of warlords and powerful landowners. Within this context and with interest rates as high as 100 percent, it seems impossible to conjure up any other solution to the everlasting financial predicament that the poor is trapped in, except for the complete elimination of the drug economy and the weakening of warlords' power. Certainly, this will have to accompany a carefully thought economic strategy in order to provide alternative means of subsistence to the farming population of Afghanistan.

In addition to paying high rent, many also have to make illegal tax payments to the police and other state officials at rates as high as $1000 per month.[96] Undoubtedly, this illicit stream of income helps warlords and corrupt government officials maintain

---

[93] As an example, see: Heffernan, John and Jennifer Leaning. "Warlords' Crimes: Secrets of an Afghan grave." International Herald Tribune February 9, 2004
<http://www.iht.com/articles/2004/02/09/edheffer_ed3_.php>.

[94] See report by Afghanistan Independent Human Rights Commission (AIHRC) on "Economic and Social Rights in Afghanistan," May 2006: p. 8.

[95] For more information on Afghan agriculture, see: Air Force Office of Special Investigations
<http://www.osi.andrews.af.mil/library/deploymentstress/otherlinks/afghanistan/economy/agriculture.asp>.

[96] "The Opium Economy: A world Awash in Heroin." The Economist Jun 28, 2007
<http://www.economist.com/research/articlesBySubject/PrinterFriendly.cfm?story_id=9409154>.

their private militia forces. Money from the bribery and extortion also helps cover expenses for their political campaigns and costs of creating networking opportunities.

The main point is that in order to survive, farmers have become dependent on harvesting poppy, and therefore been forced to rely on warlords, to whom they continuously remain in debt for protection and credit. They linger in a web of illegal economic system within which there seems to be no opportunity for exit. In circumstances as such, where there exists a severe shortage of resources, generally the poor suffers the most.

Furthermore, the manner in which farmers are involved in drug economy creates a great challenge for the opium eradication campaign. According to the United Nations Office on Drugs and Crime, in 2006 after eradication, 24.3% of farmers reported that they were not able to repay their loans. An additional 21.3% claimed that they are unable to feed their family because of the loss of their crops after eradication.[97] This means that the campaign is unlikely to be successful alienating the majority poor peasant population. The farming community would most likely seek assistance not from a weak, corrupt, and under-funded state, but from the rich, feared and powerful warlords.

With enormous economic, military, and political advantage, warlords are capable of employing both methods, namely carrot and stick to ensure the local population's dependency on *them*, and obedient to *their* rule and not to that of the state. They employ tactics that help maintain a strong grip on the private use of violence as a key tool for governance in the absence of action by the state. For example, attempting to collect debt from the poor, they resort to acts of violence such as kidnapping, forced marriages, looting, arbitrary arrest or detention and confiscation of private property (including compulsory land purchase).[98] As clear manifestation of injustice and lawlessness, the warlords, the dishonest public officials and drug traffickers pervasively practice violent methods to intimidate civilians into obedience and cooperation. This sends a clear and loud message to the Afghans: The state lacks the capacity to govern. In order to prove legitimate, it would have to produce a belief among the public that only the state is the appropriate power deserving to rule, distributing resources, and protecting the public's life and liberties in return for compliance and collaboration from the people. So far, the Afghan state has not been able to produce this outcome adequately.

Through trapping many farmers into financial obligations difficult or impossible to manage, and then exhibiting willingness to compromise by, for instance, extending a loan term to the next season, warlords have successfully established a patron-client relationship with farmers. Under these circumstances, the peasants are in debt to their creditors for the initial offer of credit. Moreover, creditors provide the cooperating

---

[97] Visit <http://www.unodc.org/afg>>. to view the executive summary of this report: "Afghanistan Opium Survey 2006."

[98] See: "Afghanistan: Country Report on Human Rights Practices." U.S. Department of State: The Bureau of Democracy, Human Rights and Labor February 28, 2005 <http://www.state.gov/g/drl/rls/hrrpt/2004/41737.htm>.

farmers with the security as well as other resources such as water, land, seed and cash to sustain a livelihood. In return, drug cultivation continues and farmers remain loyal and accommodating to traffickers. While making rational choices, the necessity to survive as well as the desire and obligation to keep one's family alive takes precedence over the loyalty to the state or adherence to morally desirable principles.

Conclusion

On one hand, the state has waged a war against terrorism, and drugs, while trying to rebuild Afghanistan. On the other, at virtually all levels within its apparatus, it has employed those who have clearly inhibited its efforts to achieve every one of these goals. This situation serves as the perfect context for the Afghan proverb: *The wolf is in charge of shepherding the heard.* This political reality severely affects equitable economic growth, security conditions, and political stability in Afghanistan. The state is entangled in a dilemma where often its policy and actions have directly clashed with its objectives. It is therefore safe to conclude that the legitimacy of the state has been gravely harmed by the pronounced military, economic and political presence of warlords in Afghanistan. Representing the state, their illegal activities have hampered the government's efforts to demonstrate functional effectiveness, as well as moral justification (two central elements signifying the notion of legitimacy) for its rule.

The previous chapter discussed how drug trade has added fuel to the fire of corruption engulfing key public institutions. This chapter has demonstrated that drug economy has substantially contributed to the creation of a politically unstable environment in which the rich becomes richer while the poor continues to suffer. This reality could partially explain the results of the United Nations' survey on poverty in Afghanistan, which has ranked this country as one of the poorest and least developed nations in the world. It could also serve as the basis for people's disgruntlement with and distrust of the state.

Since most farmers face grave resource deficiency, they rely on warlords and traffickers for obtaining support, credit, and other needed essentials. Nevertheless, this dependency is not purely economic. People cooperate with warlords not only to win the battle against poverty, but also to ensure the security of their lives. A deeper understanding of this issue helps explain President Karzai's announcement of the Jihad against farming poppy. In October 2004, he attempted to appeal to the public's religious sentiments hoping to win their support in the war on drugs campaign.[99] Warning against the dangers of drugs, he stated, "If we don't destroy drugs, drugs will destroy us."[100] In addition to destructive social ills, poppy has weakened the state on political, economic and military fronts, threatening not only its credibility but also its existence.

Although President Karzai has placed a great deal of importance and urgency on the necessity of poppy elimination repeatedly, Afghanistan continues to fall hostage in

---

[99] See "Karzai Declares Jihad on Poppy cultivation" by ABC Online: <www.abc.net.au/news>.

[100] See "H.E. President Karzai Launches the Next Phase of Afghanistan's Battle Against Illegal Drugs." Aug 22, 2006. <http://www.gov.af>.

the grips of those who benefit from drug trade. They continue to sabotage the state and the international community's efforts to rescue Afghans from poverty. Numerous media reports from Afghanistan testify that by taking advantage of the new democratic process, many involved in the upper strata of the drug industry have also deepened their roots in state institutions. Their success has endowed them with direct as well as indirect command on critical power positions. Subsequently, this has facilitated the economic feasibility of keeping their private armed forces alert and ready. Holding military, economic and political triangle of power in a tight grip, they have attained two important objectives: 1- The dependency of the majority poor on the drug industry's elite. 2- The weakness of the state position on all three (political, economic and military) fronts relative to that of the warlords. The legitimacy of the Afghan state depends not only on its ability to serve effectively through properly implementing laws and policies, but also on how the public views its character as an authority. People question the moral justification of the state's rule, and its ability to act in the best interest of the public. Unfortunately, due to embracing self-defeating policies, the state has not achieved a high degree of legitimacy through earning the right and demonstrating the determination to govern effectively. Warlords' domination has damaged the governing capacity of the state, and diluted its credibility in the eyes of the Afghan population. Put simple, in the absence of *capacity* and *credibility*, formulating and following contradictory policies, the state has not been able to assert a high degree of legitimacy.

The nimbleness of the juggler[101] in maintaining his balance on the unicycle while keeping the three flying dragons under control won him applause and monetary rewards from the spectators. The Afghan state's ability, though, to gain the public's trust in the course of combating drugs, corruption and human rights violations depends on its dexterity and political will to synchronize policy with principle.

---

[101] See chapter three.

Works Cited

"A Call for Justice: A National Consultation on Past Human Rights Violations in
     Afghanistan." The Afghan Independent Human Rights Commission" (2004): 1-
     79. <http://www.aihrc.org.af>.
"Afghan Opium Production Likely to Increase This Year, UN Warns." UN News
     Service 3 March 2006 <http:// www.un.org/apps/news/>.
"Afghanistan Crisis Paves Way for Return of the Taliban. "Daily Telegraph 27 Jun 2006
     <http://www.telegraph.co.uk/news/main.jhtml?xml=/news/2006/06/27/wafg27.xml/>.
"Afghanistan First National Human Development Report: Security With a Human
     Face." Editor in Chief Tajbakhsh Shahrbanou. Principal Writers: Saba, Saud.
     and Zakhilwal, Omar. UNDP. February 2005
"Afghanistan Opium Survey 2006: Executive Summary." United Nations Office on
     Drugs and Crime (UNODC) September 2006.
"Afghanistan: Warlords Implicated in New Abuses." Human Rights Watch Press
     Release 29 July 2003 <http://hrw.org/press/2003/07/afghan072903.htm/>.
"Afghanistan's Karzai Wants Direct Money From London Conference." 28 Feb. 2006
     <http://www.theallineed.com/news/0601/28050407.htm/>.
"Afghanistan's Warlords and the West: A Marriage Made in Hell." RW Online 16 Nov.
     2003 <http://rwor.org/a/1219wtwafg1.html/>.
"Building on Success: The London Conference on Afghanistan." The Afghanistan
     Compact 31, Jan. – 1, Feb.
"Casting Shadows: War Crimes and Crimes Against Humanity (1978-2001)." The
     Afghanistan Justice Project 2005.
"Creepin Towards the Marketplace: Small, Though Unmistakable, Signs of Progress in
     the Private Sector." The Economist 2 Feb 2006
     <http://economist.com/World/asia/PrinterFriendly.cfm?story_id=5476154/>.
"Definition of Legitimate." Merriam-Webster Online Dictionary 1 Aug. 2006
     <http://www.webster.com/dictionary/legitimate>.
"Definition of Sovereignty." Merriam-Webster Online Dictionary 1 Aug. 2006
     <http://www.webster.com/dictionary/sovereignty>.
"Despite Assurances, Karzai Falls Short on Reforms." The Daily Star 10 Oct. 2005
     <http://www.eariana.com/ariana/eariana.nsf/allDocsArticles/6A345EA1E61D2
     C2D87257096004353E1?OpenDocument/>.
"DFID Interim Strategy for Afghanistan 2005/06 (Summary)." Department for
     International Development 2005
     <http://www.dfid.gov.uk/countries/asia/afghanistan.asp/>.
"Economic and Social Rights in Afghanistan: Summary Report." Afghanistan
     Independent Human Rights Commission May, 2006.

"Justice in Afghanistan: How to Bring War Criminals to Book." The Economist 19 Jan 2006 <http://www.economist.com/research/articlesBySubject/moreArticles.cfm?subject=Afghanistan/>.

"Karzai Declares Jihad on Poppy Cultivation." ABC Online 12 Dec. 2004

"Mohammad Qasim Fahim." Afghanistan Online (Biography) <http://www.afghan-web.com/bios/today/fahim.html/>.

"Mohammad Qasim Fahim." Globalsecurity.org 30 Sep. 2006 <http://www.globalsecurity.org/military/world/afghanistan/fahim.html/>.

"Senior UN Official Visits Afghanistan to Push for Counter-drug Measures." UN News Center 22 Jan. 2006 <http://www.un.org/>.

"The Opium Situation in Afghanistan as of 29 August 2005." United Nation's Office on Drugs and Crime 29 Aug. 2005.

"U.S. Report Faults Readiness of Afghanistan's Police Force." The Baltimore Sun Dec 5, 2006: <http://www.baltimoresun.com/news/>.

"US Tells Afghan Warlords Security Needed for Aid." Daily Times 3 Nov. 2002 <http://www.dailytimes.com.pk/default.asp?page=story_3-11-2002_pg4_15/>.

"Afghan Security: Efforts to establish army and police have made progress, but future plans need to be better defined." Report to the Committee on International Relations, House of Representatives United States Government Accountability Office GAO-05-575 June/2005

"Freedom in the World: Afghanistan." Freedom House (2005) <http://www.freedomhouse.org/inc/content/pubs/fiw/inc_country_detail.cfm?year=200&country=6679&pf>.

"Karzai Calls on Taliban to Join Reconciliation Process." Swissinfo.org 12 Nov 2005. <http://www.swissinfo.org/sen/swissinfo.html?siteSect=143&sid=6233623&cKey=1131790816000>.

"Karzai Picks Dostam to Command Army." Daily Times 2 Mar. 2005. <http://www.dailytimes.com.pk/default.asp?page=story_2-3-2005_pg4_16>.

"Multi-Multi-Party Democracy: The New Parliament is a mixed Bag." The Economist 22 Oct. 2005. <www.economist.com>.

< http://news.bbc.co.uk/2/hi/south_asia/4606174.stm>.

<http://www.abc.net.au/news/newsitems/200412/s1261911.htm/>.

<www.mindfully.org/Reform/2005/AfghanistanHumanDevelopment21feb05.htm>.

Abrashi, Fisnik. "Afghan Opium Cultivation Hits a Record." Washington Post 16 Aug. 2006 <http://www.washingtonpost.com/wp-dyn/content/article/2006/08/16/AR2006081600771.html/>.

Ayazi, Akbar. "Afghanistan: President Karzai Discusses Worsening Security." Radio Free Europe 9 Nov. 2006 <http://www.rferl.org/featuresarticle/2006/11/1a8dff61-de50-4525-9042-cbbbf1dc88cb.html/>.

Baldauf, Scott. "Afghan Military Tied to Drug Trade." Christian Science Monitor 4 Sep. 2003 <http://www.csmonitor.com/2003/0904/p06s01-wosc.html>.

Barnard, Anne, and Farah Stockman. "US Weighs Role in Heroin War in Afghanistan." The Boston Globe 20 Oct. 2004 <http://www.boston.com/news/world/articles/2004/10/20/us_weighs_role_in_he roin_war_in_afghanistan/>.

Biswas, Soutik. "Puzzle of The Stay-Away Voters." BBC News, Kabul 26 Oct. 2005. <http://news.bbc.co.uk/2/hi/in_depth/south_asia/2004/afghanistan>.

Boit, John. "As Opium Poppies Flourish, Karzai's Resolve Seems to Wilt." The Baltimore Sun 22 Nov. 2006 <http://www.Baltimoresun.com/>.

Carpenter, Ted Galen. "How the Drug War in Afghanistan Undermines America's War on Terror." Foreign Policy Briefing 84. (10 Nov. 2004): 1-8.

Chandra, Vishal. "Warlords, Drugs and the 'War on Terror' in Afghanistan: The Paradoxes." Institute for Defense Studies and Analyses 30.1 (Jan-Mar 2006): 64-92.

Chu, Henry. "Afghan Amnesty Shows Warlord's Clout." Los Angeles Times 29 April 2007. 1-3. <http://www.eariana.com/ariana/eariana.nsf/allDocs/4ABC873F139B48FC8725 72CC004168A2?OpenDocument>.

Claessen, Henri J. M. "Changing Legitimacy." State Formation and Political Legitimacy: Political Anthropology, Volume VI. Ed. Ronald Cohen and Judith Toland D. New Brunswick and Oxford: Transaction Books, 1988. 23-44.

Coghlan, Tom. "Afghan MP Says She Will not be Silenced." BBC News 27 Jan. 2006.

Curtis, Grant. "Afghanistan's Opium Economy." ADB Review Dec. 2005 <http://www.adb.org/Documents/Periodicals/ADB_Review/2005vo137-6/opium-economy.asp/>.

Cusick, James. "Afghanistan: The New Drug War." Common Sense for Drug policy 29 Jan 2006 <http://www.mapinc.org/newscsdp/v06/n124/a01.html/>.

Delesues, Lorenzo, and Yama Torabi. "Reconstruction National Integrity Survey: Afghanistan 2007." The National Integrity System <http://www.tiri.org/dmdocuments/RNISS%20Afghanistan.pdf>.

Duparcq, Emmanuel. "Northern Afghan Warlords Hope for Ballots Not Bullets Ahead of Elections." Daily Times 28 Mar. 2005.

Ellis, Eric. "Karzai: One Term is Enough." Fortune Magazine 8 Aug. 2006 <http://money.cnn.com/2006/08/07/news/international/karzai.fortune/index.htm/>

Ewans, Martin. Afghanistan: A Short History of Its People and Politics. New York: Perennial, 2002.

Gall, Carlotta. "Afghan Poppy Growing Reaches Record Level, U.N. Says." New York Times 19 Nov. 2004 <http://www.nytimes.com/2004/11/19/international/asia/19afghanistan.html?ex =1258606800&%2338;en=621adc9332929eb9&%2338;ei=5088/>.

Gardiner, Beth. "World Pledges $10.5b for Afghanistan Aid." Common Sense for Drug Policy (Associated Press) 1 Feb 2006 <http://www.mapinc.org/newscsdp/v06/n138/a10.html/>.

Ghani, Ashraf, Clare Lockhart., and Michael Carnahan. "Closing the Sovereignty Gap: An Approach to State-Building." <u>Overseas Development Institute</u> (Working Paper 253) Sep. 2005.

Goodman, Jonathan. "Frontiers and Wars: The Opium Economy in Afghanistan." <u>Journal of Agrarian Change</u> (2005): 5.2 191-216.

Guimond, Laura. "The Woman Who Defies Warlords." <u>World Pulse Magazine</u> 27 June 2006 <http://www.worldpulsemagazine.com/issues/1/the_woman_who_defies_warlords/>.

Gwertzman, Bernard. "Rubin: U.S. Must Confront Warlords, Deal With Taliban." <u>Council on Foreign Relations</u> 14 July 2004. <http://www.cfr.org/publication/7191/rubin.html>.

Gwertzman, Bernard. Interview with Barnett R. Rubin. "Rubin: U.S. Must Confront Warlords, Deal Taliban." <u>Council on Foreign Relations</u> 14 July 2004.

Harnden, Toby. "Drug Trade Reaches to Afghan Cabinet." <u>The Telegraph</u> 5 Feb 2006 <http://www.telegraph.co.uk/news/main.jhtml?xml=/news/2006/02/05/wafg05.xml/>.

Ibrahimi, Sayed Y. "Officials Fired for Drug Links." <u>Afghan News Network</u> 30 Jan. 2006 <http://www.afghannews.net/printer.php?action=show&type=news&id=104/>.

Ingalls, James. "Afghanistan: The First Puppet Regime in the Post September 11 World." Presentation at the Afghan Women's Mission Conference, <u>Z Magazine</u> 30 Oct. 2002 <http://www.zmag.org/content/showarticle.cfm?ItemID=2565/>.

Ingalls, James. "The New Afghan Constitution: A Step Backwards for Democracy." <u>Foreign Policy in Focus</u> March 2004. <http://www.fpif.org/papers/2004afghanconst.html/>.

Jackson, Robert H., and Carl G. Roberg. "Why Africa's Weak States Persist: The Empirical and the Juridical in Statehood." <u>The State and Development in the Third World</u>. Ed. Atul Kohli. Princeton UP, 1986. 259-282.

Jalali, Ali A. "The Future of Afghanistan." <u>Parameters, US Army War College Quarterly</u> Spring 2006, 4-19. <http://www.carlisle.army.mil/usawc/Parameters/06spring/jalali.htm/>.

Jefferson, Thomas. "The unanimous Declaration of the thirteen united States of America." July 4, 1776 < http://www.ushistory.org/declaration/document/>.

Jones, Ann. "US Afghan Policies Going up in Smoke." <u>Asia Times</u> 2 Nov. 2006 <http://www.atimes.com/atimes/South_Asia/HK01Df01.html/>.

Karzai, Hamed. "Consolidation of Peace in Afghanistan." Tokyo Conference II. Tokyo, Japan. 5 July 2006.

Karzai, Hekmat. "Central Asia Speaks: Afghanistan's War on Drug." <u>Newscentralasia.com</u> 2 June 2006 <http://www.modules.php?name=news&file=article&sid=1296>.

Kolhatkar, Sonali, and Jim Ingalls. "Giving Democracy a Bad Name: Afghanistan's Parliamentary Elections." <u>Foreign Policy in Focus</u> 16 Sep. 2005. <http://www.fpif.org/fpiftxt/647>.

Migdal, Joel. S. "The State in Society: An Approach to Struggles for Domination. <u>"State Power and Social Forces: Domination and Transformation in the Third World</u> Ed. Joel S. Migdal, Atul Kohli, and Vivienne Shue. Cambridge UP, 1994. 1-34.

Mili. Hayder, and Jacob Townsed. "Global Terrorism Analysis: Afghanistan's Drug Trade and How it Funds Taliban Operations." The Jamestown Foundation May 10, 2007. Vol. 5, Issue 9.

Millen, Raymond A. "Afghanistan: Reconstituting a Collapsed State. "Strategic Studies Institute of the U.S. Army War College April 2005 <http://www.carlisle.army.mil/ssi/>.

Montero, David. "Corruption Eroding Afghan Security." Christian Science Monitor 28 April 2006 <http://www.csmonitor.com/2006/0428/p07s02-wosc.htm/>.

Moor, Simon Cameron. "Getting Desperate: Afghanistan Mulls Forming Militias." Reuters 11 June 2006 <http://www.washingtonpost.com/wpdyn/content/article/2006/06/11/AR200606 1100117_pf.html/>.

Naji, Meena. "Democracy in Afghanistan? An Authoritarian State is in the Process of Construction." Counter Currents 25 Feb 2004 <http://www.countercurrents.org/afghan-nanji250204.htm/>.

"News and Analysis: Two Former Taliban Win Seats in Afghan parliament." Radio Free Europe 25 Oct. 2005. <http://www.rferl.org/en/specials/elections/features/2005/10/5763D47B-235A-4699-B050-ACBA12A32967.ASP>.

Ottaway, Marina., and Anatol Lieven. "Rebuilding Afghanistan: Fantasy Versus Reality." Carnegie Endowment for International Peace: Policy Brief 12 Jan. 2002.

Pan, Esther. "Afghanistan: Karzai vs. Warlords." Council on Foreign Relations 15 Sep. 2004 <http://www.cfr.org/publication/7791/afghanistan.html/>.

Pan, Esther. "Afghanistan: Karzai vs. the Warlords." Council on Foreign Relations 15 Sep 2004. http://www.cfr.org/publication/7791/afghanistan.html

Popal, Ajmal. "Jabbar Sabet on a Trip to London." Kabul Press 15 Nov. 2006 <http://kabulpress.org/maghala_23aghrabe85.htm>.

Rodgers, Jimmie. "Democracy and Terrorism." AOL Journals 15 Mar. 2005.

Rohde, David., And David E. Sanger, "How a 'Good War' in Afghanistan Went Bad." New York Times Aug. 12, 2007. <http://www.nytimes.com>.

Rubin, Barnett R. "(Re)Building Afghanistan: The Folly of Stateless Democracy." Current History 103. Jan-Dec 2004, 165.

Rubin, Barnett R. "Road to Run: Afghanistan's Booming Opium Industry." Center on International Cooperation & Center for American Progress 7 Oct. 2004.

Rubin, Barnett R., and Armstrong, Andrea. "Regional Issues in the Reconstruction of Afghanistan." Center on International Cooperation Conflict Prevention Recovery and Peace Building. <http://www.cic.nyu.edu/pdf/wpj_afghanistan.pdf>.

Rubin, Barnett R., and Omar Zakhilwal. "A War on Drugs, or a War on Farmers?" The Wall Street Journal 11 Jan. 2005, Eastern Ed. A20.

Rubin, Barnett. R. The Fragmentation of Afghanistan: State Formation and Collapse in the International System. Yale University Press: New Haven: Yale University Press, 2002.

Schar, John H., "Legitimacy in the Modern State." Ed. William Connolly <u>Legitimacy and the State</u> New York: New York UP, 1984. 104-133.

Schroen, Gary C. <u>First In: An Insider's Account of How the CIA Spearheaded the War on Terror in Afghanistan</u>. New York: Ballantine Books, 2005.

Sedra, Mark. And Peter Middlebrook. "Beyond Bonn: Provisioning the International Compact for Afghanistan." <u>Foreign Policy in Focus (FPIF)</u> Nov. 2005 1-24. <http://www.fpif.org/>.

Shishkin, Philip. "Heavy Traffic in Afghanistan: Heroin Trade Soars Despite U.S. Aid." <u>Common Sense for Drug Policy</u> 18 Jan 2006 <http://www.mapinc.org/newscsdp/v06/n078/a07.html/>.

Smith, Graeme. "Opium-Planting Time." <u>The Globe and Mail</u> 3 Oct. 2005 <http://www.theglobeandmail.com/servlet/ArticleNews/TPStory/LAC/2005100 3/OPIUM03/TPInternational/TopStories>.

Suhrke, Astri. "When More is Less: Aiding Statebuilding in Afghanistan." <u>The C. Michelson Institute</u> 25 Oct. 2006 <http://www.policypointers.org/page_4352.html/>.

Svensson, Jakob. "Eight Questions About Corruption." <u>Journal of Economic Perspectives</u> 19.3 (2005): 19-42.

Synovitz, Ron. "Afghanistan: Plan to Recruit Militia as Police Sparks Concern." <u>Eurasianet.org</u> 18 June 2006 <http://www.eurasianet.org/departments/insight/articles/pp061806.shtml/>.

Tarzi, Amin. "Analysis: Afghan Demonstrations Test Warlords-Turned Administrators." <u>Radio Free Europe</u> 9 Mar. 2005 <http://www.rferl.org/featuresarticle/2005/03/3acb6349-bcb1-4d51-a8df-8a5a131d6aa0.html/>.

Weber, Max. "Legitimacy, Politics and the State: Politics as a Vocation." <u>Legitimacy and the State</u> Ed. William Connolly. New York: New York UP, 1984. 32-62.

Woodward, Bob. "CIA Led Way With Cash Handouts." <u>Washington Post</u> 18 Nov. 2002 < http://www.washingtonpost.com/wp-dyn/articles/A3105-2002Nov17.html>.

www.ingramcontent.com/pod-product-compliance
Lightning Source LLC
Chambersburg PA
CBHW052006280526
45793CB00005B/863